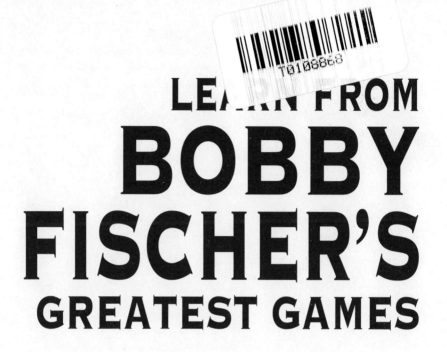

# LEARN FROM BOBBY FISCHER'S GREATEST GAMES

## ERIC SCHILLER

## CARDOZA PUBLISHING

## ABOUT THE AUTHOR

Eric Schiller, widely considered one of the world's foremost chess analysts, writers, and teachers, is internationally recognized for his definitive works on openings. He is the author of 100 chess books including Cardoza Publishing's series on openings, *Gambit Chess Openings, World Champion Openings, Standard Chess Openings, and Unorthodox Chess Openings* — an exhaustive opening library of more than 2,500 pages.

Schiller is a National and Life Master of the United States Chess Federation and hold titles of FIDE Master, International Arbiter and International Organizer from the World Chess Federation. He has coached and trained many of America's finest young players and teaches in California's schools. He has been involved in World Chess Championships as arbiter and press officer since 1983.

Schiller's web site is www.ericschiller.com. He is the senior editor of the free major chess website, www.chesscity.com.

## ACKNOWLEDGMENTS

Thanks to Chris Washburn, who was once again able to proofread the book on very short notice.

———

Cardoza Publishing is the foremost gaming publisher in the world with a library of more than 200 up-to-date and easy-to-read books and strategies. These authoritative works are written by the top experts in their fields and with more than 10,000,000 books in print, represent the best-selling and most popular gaming books anywhere.

### 2017 THIRD EDITION
Copyright © 2004, 2009, 2017 by Eric Schiller
- All Rights Reserved -

Library of Congress Catalog No: 2017948810
ISBN 13: 978-1-58042-352-6

Visit our website or write us for a full list of our books, software and advanced strategies.

———

### CARDOZA PUBLISHING
P.O. Box 98115, Las Vegas, NV 89193
Phone (800)577-WINS
email: cardozabooks@aol.com
**www.cardozabooks.com**

# TABLE OF CONTENTS

## OPENING AND MIDDLEGAME WISDOM

 # INTRODUCTION

In chess, the question of who is the greatest American player of all time is easily answered: Bobby Fischer. Bobby Fischer not only became Wo rld Champion, he changed the entire chess world in the process. Fischer's games can teach you almost anything you need to know about the game of chess. In this book, I'll show you some of these games and try to extract the nuggets of wisdom.

I present a selection of Fischer's greatest games with clear explanations of the thinking behind all of the significant moves. Unlike most collections of Fischer's games, this book does not explore alternative strategies not actually played in the game, except when necessary to demonstrate an instructive lesson. You are encouraged to enjoy the game and to absorb tips that will help provide better results at the chessboard, even if you are not gifted with Fischer's incredible chess genius.

Fischer's games have fascinated chess players for decades. Many fine books have been written that study these games in detail and try to present definitive analysis of all of the moves and alternatives.

I try to bring the beauty, grace, wisdom, and sometimes jaw-dropping amazement of Fischer's play to those who are just starting out in the game, or who have only been playing for a little while.

My goal is to present the games so that even those just starting in chess can follow the action and appreciate many of Fischer's fine moves. The explanations are presented in prose, with some chess notation. Those who've been playing chess for a little while may even be able to follow the main lines of the games without the use of a chess board, thanks to the many diagrams showing the state of play.

In each highlighted game, you'll find tips and strategies that you can apply to your own games. By playing through these games and reading the explanations I provide, you will sharpen your own chess skills. Of course, you'll still make mistakes, but then, as you will see, even the incomparable Bobby Fischer made his share of mistakes too. All chess players, even the very best, make mistakes. The goal is to learn from those mistakes and avoid repeating them.

This book is devoted to the instructional value of Fischer's games. I have not provided a great deal of biographical or historical information. Since Bobby Fischer is considered by virtually all chess players to be among the greatest of all time, there are many, many books about him. Those looking for deeper analysis than what is within these pages should consult the recommended reading list at the back of the book.

As for his off the board antics and controversies, I see no need to include them here as they only distract from the instructional value and artistic beauty of the games. That material is available in a variety of books or simply through an online search. My own brief meetings with Fischer did not provide any special insights. I want the reader to be able to concentrate on the beauty and wisdom of Fischer's actual chess moves. I hope that this book provides a pleasant and enjoyable experience of a sort previously unavailable to beginners.

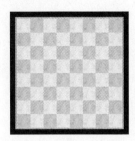

# THE TALE OF AMERICA'S GREATEST PLAYER

Wherever you go you'll find chess players and wherever you find chess players you'll find people who know of Bobby Fischer, the greatest chess player in the history of America, and without doubt one of the greatest chess players of all-time. Fischer's adventures, on and off the board, have been heavily chronicled, and all chess fans should take some time to familiarize themselves with the career of America's greatest player.

In case you haven't come across one of the fine biographies of Bobby Fischer yet, here are the basic facts: Robert James Fischer was born March 9, 1943 in Chicago, Illinois. While the world was embroiled in a war, Bobby's domestic life didn't get off to a great start. His parents separated when he was just two years old. Bobby's mother, a registered nurse, raised him, moving to Brooklyn where she was hoping to further her education. The New York area was certainly the hub of chess in the country and so it is hardly surprising that Fischer came into contact with the game at an early age. Bobby's fascination with chess began when he was just six years old. In fact, as a child, he didn't even want new friends unless they played chess. Replying to a letter from Mrs. Fischer, the venerable chess figure Herman Helms invited the Fischers to come to the chess club at the Brooklyn Public Library. He also offered an introduction to the Brooklyn Chess Club, one of the leading chess institutions of the time.

Fischer quickly made a sensational impact. In the 1954 club championship he tied for third to fifth-place even though most of his competition was several times his age. It didn't take long for Bobby to leap into the national tournament scene. In 1955 he participated in the U.S. junior championship in Nebraska, getting a respectable even score considering he was only twelve years old. In 1956 he won the U.S. junior championship in Philadelphia by winning eight games, drawing one, and dropping one.

That same year he came to the attention of the entire chess world by winning a brilliant game against Donald Byrne at the Rosenwald Memorial in New York City. This was the game that earned the title "Game of the Century," an astonishing accomplishment for a 13-year-old. A year later he not only won the U.S. Junior Championships in San Francisco, with eight wins and just one draw, but also won the U.S. Open on the other side of the country in New Jersey, with eight wins and four draws. Next he won a tournament in New Jersey on his way to the stunning achievement of winning the United States championship, held in New York City, with eight wins, five draws and no losses.

In 1958 it was time for major international competition and he was invited to a qualifying stage for the World Championship. The tournament, known as an Interzonal, was held in Portotoz, Yugoslavia. Despite the chattel and new experiences of being in Yugoslavia, he managed a very impressive tie for fifth and sixth place. Then he came back to New York and won the U.S. championship again, something that turned out to be quite routine for him. He did it again in 1959, 1960, and 1962. In that year (1958) Fischer won the Interzonal tournament in Stockholm, qualifying to move on to a tournament of World Championship candidates in Curacao. He finished fourth in that event, and then went off to win the U.S. championship yet again.

In 1963, Bobby achieved a result never matched in the history of American chess. He not only won the United States championship again, he won all eleven games: no draws, no defeats! To win a twelve player tournament with a perfect score is an almost impossible achievement, especially when all of the opponents are qualified chess masters. The next year Bobby participated in the Casablanca Memorial Tournament in Havana, one of the strongest annual tournaments. He was not allowed to travel to Cuba so he had to play by teletype, sitting at a board in the Marshall Chess Club in New York City. Even so, he managed to tie for second place.

It was time to make a serious bid for the World Championship. In 1966 he took on many of the world's top players in the famous Piatigorski Cup in Santa Monica, California. He finished second there, and then dominated the chess Olympiad in Havana (this time the Americans received State Department clearance to travel) scoring fourteen wins, two draws, and only a single loss. Next, it was off to win yet another United States championship in New York. The stage was set for him to participate in a qualifying phase for the 1969 World Championship. That started with the Interzonal tournament in Sousse, Tunisia. Things were going quite well, but, after winning seven games and drawing three, Bobby withdrew from the event. Though he won every tournament he played in 1967, 1968, and 1970 (he barely played in 1969), he had to sit on the sidelines as Boris Spassky won the World Championship title from Tigran Petrosian.

Fortunately, in 1970 he was able to participate in the Interzonal tournament in Palma de Mallorca, Spain. He tore through the field, winning fifteen games, drawing seven and losing only two to take first place. Now he had to defeat three players in individual matches before he could challenge Spassky. Fischer not only achieved the goal, but he did so in a way that has never been duplicated and almost certainly never will. He smashed Mark Taimanov, a top Russian player, 6-0 with no draws. This remarkable achievement was followed by shutting out Bent Larson, the highly talented Danish player, by the same score. Against Tigran Petrosian — the World Champion who held the title until Spassky took it away — he did lose one game, but won five and drew three to easily take the match. The stage was set for the dramatic confrontation between the famous Russian Boris Spassky, World Champion from the Soviet Union, and Bobby Fischer, the brash, unpredictable American.

When Bobby defeated Spassky by winning seven, drawing eleven, and losing three, he drew attention from the entire world. The Communist side in the Cold War considered themselves invulnerable at the chess board. A single American smashed this notion, and although Russia has continued to more or less dominate the world chess scene, the domination could never again be complete. Of the first ten World Champions, the Soviet Union had produced five in a row. The defeat was a major psychological blow to the Soviet government. Bobby Fischer had clobbered the Soviet "army."

In a dispute over regulations for his title defense, Bobby had the title taken away from him by the World Chess Federation. He did not show up to defend his title and so it went to the winner of the Candidates' Match between two Russian players. As a result, Anatoly Karpov became the twelfth World Champion. Unfortunately Karpov never played Fischer. Bobby went into self-imposed exile from the game, not to play chess for twenty years.

In 1992, Bobby did play a match against his old nemesis Boris Spassky and defeated him handily. He hasn't played a public game since and it is not expected that he will ever return to a public chess board. And that's just a sketch of a Bobby's career. There are so many fascinating elements that large books have been written just describing his path through life. The magnificent book by Frank Brady, Bobby Fischer: Profile of Prodigy, is the best place to start if you really want to get to know Bobby Fischer, the man.

In this book you will see some of Bobby's best games, and learn important chess lessons. But if you're a fan of chess, you owe it to yourself to discover more about this fascinating American champion. Even now, in retirement, the subject of Fischer dominates many chess discussions. It is a pity this discussion involves not the moves Bobby has made on the chess board, but rather the outrageous comments he has made. I am going to stick to looking at the brilliant, instructive play of the greatest American ever to play the game.

# OPENING
# AND
# MIDDLEGAME
# WISDOM

**GAME #1**

# THE GAME
# OF THE CENTURY

**THE PLAYERS**
Bobby Fischer (Black)
vs.
Donald Byrne (U.S.A.)

**THE LOCATION**
The Rosenwald Memorial,
in New York, U.S.A.,
on 10/17/1956

## LESSON: THE FOUR RULES OF THE OPENING

An experienced player should aim for four goals.

1. You want a pawn, or two, in the center of the board (e4, d4, e5, d5).
2. Your king must be castled to safety.
3. Your rooks should be able to see each other (no pieces in the way).
4. At least one rook should take up a position on an open line, preferably on the d-file or e-file.

Although it isn't necessary to do these in a particular order, beginners should generally use them in the order of the list. Sometimes you may want to move a rook to the center before moving out all of the knights and bishops.

The process of mobilizing your forces and getting them into position is known as "development." Your development is complete when you have castled and the two rooks are connected.

**1.Nf3.** The game begins with a flexible move that can lead to just about any opening. Although White does not place a pawn in the center, there is no way to stop that from happening on the next move. Black can place a pawn at d5, but moving a pawn to e5 requires preparation. **1...Nf6.** Fischer similarly refuses to disclose his intentions. However, he takes away any possibility of White getting a second pawn to the center at e4, at least for a few moves. **2.c4 g6 3.Nc3 Bg7 4.d4 O-O 5.Bf4 d5.**

Now we reach the Gruenfeld Defense by transposition. Both sides have a pawn in the center. Black has already castled, and only three moves are needed before the rooks will see each other.

**6.Qb3.** Byrne chooses to play a Russian strategy, one of the richest and most interesting variations available to White. **6...dxc4;7.Qxc4.** In the Russian Variations, Black has many defensive schemes. White's move order, playing Bf4 before e4, avoids some of them. **7...c6; 8.e4.** White has the ideal pawn center, and it is up to Black to destroy it. **8...Nbd7.** 8...b5; 9.Qb3! Qa5; 10.Bd3 Be6; 11.Qd1 Rd8; 12.O-O Bg4; 13.e5 Nd5; 14.Nxd5 cxd5; 15.Rc1 was played in Miles vs. Kasparov, Basel (2nd match game) 1985. After 15...Qb6, Kasparov obtained a small advantage with 16.Rc5, but could have gotten even more with 16.e6! The alternative 9...Be6; 10.Qc2 Qa5 is Kasparov's suggestion for Black.

**9.Rd1 Nb6; 10.Qc5.** This seems to be an odd location for the queen, but in fact it is seen in many examples of the Russian

Variation. She can be driven back by moving a knight to d7, but that only gets in the way of the other Black pieces.

**10...Bg4.** Black uses a threat on the knight at f3 to place indirect pressure on the pawn at d4. **11.Bg5?** It is generally unwise to reposition pieces that are already in the game until you have castled. White's move is effectively an admission that he's already made a mistake. The other bishop should have entered the game. **11...Na4.** If White captures 12.Nxa4, then Black grabs the e-pawn with 12...Nxe4!, attacking the White queen. The queen can eat the pawn at e7, but after 13.Qxe7 Qa5+ White is in trouble. The open e-file, leading to the White king, is a real problem. **12.Qa3.** As usual in the Gruenfeld, Black's action is at c3, d4 and e4. The fun begins now. **12...Nxc3; 13.bxc3 Nxe4; 14.Bxe7.**

Black offers a rook for the White bishop. Trading a rook for a bishop or a knight is known as "an exchange," which is one of chess's more confusing phrases. In some languages they use a word which means "quality," which is a bit better. The idea is that the rook is worth more than the bishop, so it isn't an even trade. Traditionally, the rook is worth five units and the bishop only three. This is a simplistic generalization that is largely ignored by advanced players. Here, the invading dark-squared bishop is far too valuable to give up for the relatively inactive rook at f8.

**14...Qb6; 15.Bc4 Nxc3.** Mission accomplished! White cannot capture the knight at c3 because then Black can move a rook to e8 to pin the bishop. **16.Bc5 Rfe8+.** White is forced to abandon castling and Black has threats against all three back-rank squares. The rook at e8 controls e1, the knight can come to d2 to attack g1, and the bishop can swing from g4 to the queenside, where the a6-f1 diagonal can be used. The key to White's hopes is the powerful defensive ability of the bishop at c4. **17.Kf1.**

**17...Be6!!** A truly stunning move. In return for the queen, Black gets access to all the critical squares. **18.Bxb6.** 18.Bxe6 just draws in the powerful White queen. 18...Qb5+; 19.Kg1 Ne2+; 20.Kf1 Ng3+; 21.Kg1 and the end comes with the famous smothered mate. 21...Qf1+; 22.Rxf1 Ne2. Checkmate.

**18...Bxc4+; 19.Kg1 Ne2+.** This knight cannot give checkmate, but it can inflict mortal damage. **20.Kf1 Nxd4+; 21.Kg1 Ne2+; 22.Kf1 Nc3+; 23.Kg1 axb6.** Now Black has two pieces and two pawns for the queen, with the White queen and rook under attack and the rook at h1 locked out of the game.

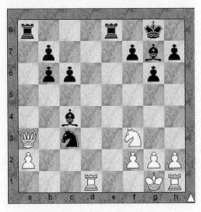

**24.Qb4 Ra4!; 25.Qxb6 Nxd1; 26.h3.** This creates a new home for the king, so that the rook can enter the game. **26...Rxa2.** A rook on the seventh rank is a mighty attacking force, and without moving until the very end of the game, it leads the attacking forces. **27.Kh2 Nxf2.**

**28.Re1 Rxe1; 29.Qd8+ Bf8; 30.Nxe1 Bd5.** This position is an easy win for Black, who has a rook, two bishops and three pawns for the queen. **31.Nf3 Ne4; 32.Qb8.** The queen is out of play here, so Fischer will be able to use his massive forces to checkmate the White king.

**32...b5; 33.h4 h5; 34.Ne5 Kg7.** Black unpins the bishop at f8. It will play a leading role in the attack. **35.Kg1 Bc5+; 36.Kf1 Ng3+; 37.Ke1 Bb4+; 38.Kd1 Bb3+.**

Black's bishops are simply overpowering, especially when combined with a rook on the 7th rank. **39.Kc1 Ne2+; 40.Kb1 Nc3+; 41.Kc1 Rc2. Checkmate.**

**Game notes:** This game was awarded the Brilliancy Prize for the tournament. It has been called "The Game of the Century" for good reason. It is an absolutely incredible performance by a thirteen year-old future World Champion!

# GAME #2

# OWN THE CENTER, DOMINATE THE BOARD

**THE PLAYERS**
Bobby Fischer (White)
vs.
James Sherwin (U.S.A.)

**THE LOCATION**
New Jersey Open Championship,
in East Orange, New Jersey,
U.S.A., on 9/2/1957

## LESSON: CONTROLLING THE CENTER OF THE BOARD HELPS WHEN YOU ATTACK ON THE FLANK!

The chessboard is a battlefield. Although the board is flat, it is important to think of the center (e4, e5, d4, d5) as a platform offering excellent views. From the center of the board, pieces, even slow-moving knights, can get to either side of the board quickly.

If you put your pieces in the center of the board, they are subject to attack from enemy forces. That's why you have to try to control as much of the center as possible. If you have pawns in the center, they can not only defend your other pieces, but also guard squares so that enemy forces can't use them.

It is often said, wisely, that the best way to counter a flank attack is to counterattack in the center. To prevent that, control the center when attacking on either side, so that the opponent can't mount the necessary central operations. Study of the different types of center is a rather advanced topic. Beginners should just remember to keep an eye on it. Don't let your opponent seize control of the center, even if you can't dominate it yourself.

**1.e4 c5; 2.Nf3 e6; 3.d3.** Normally, White moves the pawn to d4 here. Fischer decides to play a "closed" system. There will be no early skirmishes. Both players will get their pieces into the game before the real battles begin. **3...Nc6; 4.g3 Nf6; 5.Bg2.** The formation on the kingside is known as a "fianchetto." The bishop sits inside the triangle of pawns, defending important squares at f3 and h3 that were weakened when the pawn moved up to g3. The bishop can eventually operate along the a8-h1 diagonal, but should generally remain in place for defensive purposes. **5...Be7; 6.O-O O-O; 7.Nbd2.**

The knight moves to this square, temporarily, because the natural home at c3 is destined to be occupied by a pawn. **7...Rb8.** Fischer remarked that Sherwin slid the rook to this square with his pinky, as if to emphasize the mystery of the move. It isn't the best, however. In 1967, the Mongolian player Miagmarsuren showed a better plan against Bobby at the Interzonal Tournament in Sousse, Tunisia.

7...d5 is the natural move in the Sicilian Defense. In this case, play would take place in the French Defense, which normally starts 1.e4 e6. The game against Miagmarsuren continued 8.Re1 b5; 9.e5 Nd7; 10.Nf1 b4; 11.h4 a5 with play on opposite wings. The position is satisfactory for both players, who can attack at will. If White cannot take out the enemy king, Black's queenside advances will soon lead to a superior game.

**8.Re1 d6; 9.c3.** This is played to prepare the advance of the d-pawn to d4. Then, if it is captured by Black's c-pawn, White will be able to recapture with the pawn.

**9...b6; 10.d4.** This establishes the "ideal pawn center." The pawns in the center control many important squares along the fifth rank. Black can't use those squares to maneuver pieces. White uses a strategy of attacking on the kingside, since Black cannot easily maneuver forces into defensive positions.

**10...Qc7?!** With this move, Black evacuates the d-file and prepares to transfer a rook to d8, to support action in the center. The queen adds support to d5, which is already covered by the knight at c6 and pawn at d6. But White, with a pawn at d4, rook at e1 and knight at f3, has equal influence there.

The game might have seen 10...cxd4; 11.cxd4 and now Fischer proposed 11...d5. Huebner's 11...Bb7 would lead to a modern style position with pressure against White's center. When the game was played, such an approach would have been considered too much of a concession.

**11.e5!** Fischer takes control of e5, and chases the knight from f6. This means that the kingside pawns are defended only by the king himself. That's always a dangerous situation. **11...Nd5.** If the knight retreats to d7, then White uses the same strategy seen in the game, and it is even worse for Black, since the knight is awkwardly placed. Sherwin might have tried capturing the pawn and then retreating the knight. **12.exd6 Bxd6; 13.Ne4!** Black is faced with a dilemma. There are no good options.

**13...c4.** 13...Be7; 14.c4 Nf6; 15.Bf4 skewers Black's queen and rook. 13...cxd4; 14.Nxd6 Qxd6; 15.c4! Nf6 (or ...Nde7); 16.Bf4 is a variation on the same theme. **14.Nxd6 Qxd6.** Black has parted with the useful dark square bishop and is left with a "bad bishop" at c8. Perhaps the remaining bishop can be used on the a8-h1 diagonal, eventually, but Black can't afford slow plans if his kingside is under attack. So Bobby starts to move in for the kill. **15.Ng5!** The knight stares menacingly at h7.

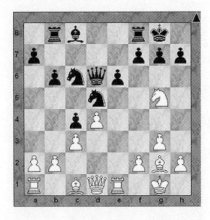

**15...Nce7?** Sherwin rushes his knight to the kingside to help with the defense. In general, this is a wise strategy. In this particular position, Black should kick out the invading knight right away. **16.Qc2!** The queen is a long range piece and can attack as effectively from c2 as from h5, where it might get chased away by ...Nf6. Fischer threatens immediate checkmate at h7. **16...Ng6; 17.h4.** The pawn plays a major role in the attack. It threatens to chase the enemy knight from g6, allowing checkmate at h7. **17... Nf6.**

**18.Nxh7!** Fischer does not hesitate to sacrifice the knight. He was able to calculate all the possible defenses, of course. For mere mortals, the calculations might be difficult, but all you really need to see is that Black will not be able to control f4, and that means that White will get a bishop there and win material at some point. **18...Nxh7; 19.h5.** The knight must move and White gains access to the critical square. **19...Nh4; 20.Bf4 Qd8.** White could now simply capture the rook at b8, but then Black would eliminate the bishop at g2 and White's king might find himself in some danger. Fischer is intent on a kingside attack, and cannot be bought off by mere material.

**21.gxh4! Rb7!** A clever move. Black offers the rook to the White bishop at g2. This bishop is needed for defense, so Bobby resists the temptation and continues with the attack. **22.h6!** Black is faced with a difficult decision. Bobby does have a way of making opponents feel uncomfortable!

**22...Qxh4.** 22...g6; 23.h5 is hopeless. 22...f5 is proposed by Huebner but after 23.Bxb7 Bxb7; 24.f3! White can bring the queen to defend the kingside, and the consequences of capturing at f3 are disastrous. 24...Bxf3; 25.Re3! Be4; 26.Qh2 and soon the rook at a1 will join the battle and finish things off.

**23.hxg7!** The second of the three barrier pawns is removed. Black is going to have to defend the king with more important pieces. **23...Kxg7?** Black missed a trick here. By moving the rook to d8, the White pawn could be used as a shield against attack! Sometimes an enemy piece can actually help defend. **24.Re4.**

Fischer uses a "rook lift" to get the rook to a position where it can join the attack. Once the bishop moves from f4, the rook can move along the fourth rank. If Black isn't careful, the game will be over quickly after the bishop moves to e5 with check. Black has to do something about the check, so White will then capture the queen at h4. This tactic is known as a "discovered attack." **24...Qh5; 25.Re3.** Since Sherwin didn't fall for the trick, and still covers g4, the rook slides back, ready to slip over to the g-file or h-file. **25... f5.** This move is necessary to enable the king to flee to the center without leaving the knight at h7 subject to attack. The threat was simply Rh3.

**26.Rh3 Qe8; 27.Be5+.** Once again, Fischer rejects the materialistic win of the exchange, this time via Bh6+, in favor of a continuing attack. He could have grabbed two exchanges, capturing at b7 as well. But then he wouldn't be able to use the attacking force of his bishops. In this case, the bishops are just as strong as the rooks.

**27...Nf6.** The only move. 27...Kg8 is eliminated by 28.Rg3+ Kf7; 29.Rg7. Checkmate. **28.Qd2 Kf7; 29.Qg5 Qe7.** On 29...Ke7, 30.Rh7+ wins. The knight at f6 is pinned, so the rook cannot be captured. 30...Rf7 loses to 31.Qxf6+! Here it is the rook at f7 that is pinned by its counterpart at h7.

**30.Bxf6 Qxf6; 31.Rh7+.** White is going to pick off the Black rook at b7, after the queens come off. **31...Ke8; 32.Qxf6 Rxh7.** 32... Rxf6 33.Bxb7 Bxb7; 34.Rxb7 leaves Black a rook down. **33.Bc6+.** Sherwin resigned, because if the bishop interposes at d7, White simply plays Qxe6+ and the queen cannot be captured because the bishop is pinned.

# DEATH TO DRAGONS

**THE PLAYERS**

Bobby Fischer (White)
vs.
Bent Larsen (Denmark)

**THE LOCATION**

The Interzonal,
in Portoroz, Slovenia
on 8/16/1958

## LESSON: OPPOSITE WING CASTLING

If you prefer a peaceful contest, castle on the same side of the board as your opponent. If you are in the mood for a brawl, then placing your king on the opposite flank from your opponent is the way to go.

In the Sicilian Defence (1.e4 c5), White often castles on the queenside, while Black almost always castles on the kingside. This allows each side to attack the other using pawns. The White king, on the queenside, is not weakened when the g-pawn and h-pawn advance. Black, on the other hand, can throw the a- and b-pawns up the board, without having any worries for the king.

When kings are on opposite flanks, there usually isn't much time for patient maneuvering. The race is on, and the winner survives while the losing king dies. Sacrifices are common, and are used to accelerate the attack.

Such a fight is usually a lot of fun, at least for the winner. The winner is usually the player who can calculate more accurately. However, there is always the danger of a knockout blow which can lead to victory even for a player of limited skills. When facing a top player like Bobby Fischer, it is dangerous indeed!

**1.e4 c5; 2.Nf3 d6; 3.d4 cxd4; 4.Nxd4 Nf6; 5.Nc3 g6.**

The famous Dragon Sicilian! Bobby didn't have much respect for this exciting line. He claimed that all White had to do is open the h-file, sac a few pieces, and deliver checkmate! Well, it isn't quite that simple, and the Dragon remains a popular opening at all levels of play. The bishop will take up residence at g7 and eventually wreak havoc on the a1-h8 diagonal. If, that is, the Black king can survive a massive kingside assault.

**6.Be3 Bg7; 7.f3 O-O; 8.Qd2 Nc6; 9.Bc4.** The standard continuation, known as the Yugoslav Attack, sees queenside castling by White, so that the kingside pawns can be hurled forward without exposing the White king to attack. Black has many choices here, but Larsen adopts one that was popular at the time.

**9...Nxd4.** The exchange of knights brings the White bishop to d4, so that Black doesn't have to face an invasion at h6. These days, it is considered wiser to develop the queenside, and in particular, get a rook to c8. Later, that rook will be sacrificed for the White knight at c3, and Black will attack furiously on the queenside. 9...Bd7 is the modern preference. The knight will go to e5, and later c4, forking the White queen and bishop, so that White will have to exchange the light square bishop for it.

**10.Bxd4 Be6; 11.Bb3 Qa5; 12.O-O-O.** The problem faced by Black is that the White king enjoys the protection of two bishops, a knight, and a healthy pawn structure. Although White has no pieces directly attacking the kingside, the pawnstorm develops very quickly.

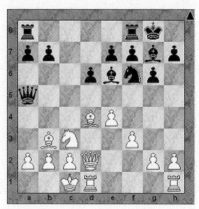

**12...b5.** This is the most active plan. Black has also successfully played 12...Rfc8. Black is not concerned about a White capture at e6, because that would get rid of a great defender, the bishop at b3. The damage to the pawn structure would not be significant.
**13.Kb1.** White almost always plays this move. It sets up a tactical threat of Nd5, since if Black captures at d2, White takes the e-pawn with check before recapturing the queen. That won't work if the king is still at c1 because the queen at d2 would be captured with check.

**13...b4; 14.Nd5 Bxd5; 15.Bxd5 Rac8.** 15...Nxd5; 16.Bxg7 leads to 16...Nc3+; 17.bxc3 Rab8. Here 18.cxb4 Qxb4+; 19.Qxb4 Rxb4+; 20.Bb2 Rfb8 was Fischer's analysis. White would lose the bishop and have an inferior endgame. 18.c4 has been played. 18... Kxg7; 19.h4 Rb6; 20.h5 Ra6; 21.Qd4+ e5; 22.Qb2 was tested in Fernandez vs. Lerch, in Catalunya, Spain, 1992, over three decades later! Black has enough pressure at a2 to survive a kingside attack, but White managed to win anyway. 16.exd5 Qxd5; 17.Qxb4, however, was what Fischer intended to play.

**16.Bb3!** Bobby keeps the valuable defender. Commenting on this position, he made his famous comment that he "had it down to a science: pry open the KR[h]-file and sac, sac ... mate!" **16... Rc7.** This move protects the a-pawn so the queen can get out of the way. Then, Black can advance the a-pawn and create his own pawn storm. **17.h4.** Here we go! **17...Qb5.** 17...h5; 18.g4 hxg4; 19.h5 leads to a decisive attack. It is fun to hand such positions to a computer, which will start out favoring Black's extra pawn, and then start realizing the danger faced by the Black king, despite the presence of two defenders. Fischer gives the line 19...gxh5; 20.fxg4 Nxe4; 21.Qe3 Nf6; 22.gxh5 e5; 23.h6 and White will win. **18.h5.**

**18...Rfc8.** Black just can't keep the h-file closed. 18...gxh5 sees the kingside ripped open with 19.g4! hxg4; 20.fxg4 Nxe4 when 21.Qh2

places Black in a hopeless situation. Fischer finishes elegantly: 21…
Ng5; 22.Bxg7 Kxg7; 23.Rd5 Rc5; 24.Qh6+ Kg8; 25.Rxg5+ Rxg5;
26.Qxh7. Checkmate.

18…Nxh5 is a tougher nut to crack, and Bobby didn't mention it.
Neither do most other analysts. The solution involves an instructive
example of a pawnstorm. 19.Bxg7 Kxg7; 20.g4 Nf6 is a typical
Dragon maneuver. 21.Qh6+ Kg8; 22.g5 wins the knight, since
Black has to shift the rook from f8 to avoid mate at h7 before the
knight can move away.

**19.hxg6 hxg6; 20.g4 a5.** The race is on. It is no contest.

**21.g5 Nh5.** 21…Ne8; 22.Bxg7 Nxg7 gets demolished, as Bobby
demonstrated: 23.Rh6! Threatening to double rooks on the h-file
and checkmate at h8 and h7. 23…e6; 24.Qh2 Nh5 where the
kingside explodes after 25.Bxe6! fxe6; 26.Rxg6+ Ng7; 27.Rh1 and
Black could resign. White also wins the race after 21…a4; 22.gxf6
axb3; 23.fxg7 bxc2+; 24.Qxc2 Rxc2; 25.Rh8. Checkmate.

**22.Rxh5!** A standard exchange sacrifice in the Dragon Variation
of the Sicilian Defense brings the game to a swift and brutal
conclusion. White can invest bits of material, since his bishop at
b3 holds off the entire enemy army! **22…gxh5; 23.g6!** Not only
does the bishop defend, it also participates in the attack by pinning
Black's f-pawn. **23…e5.** The pawn must take two steps. On 23…
e6; 24.gxf7+ Kxf7; 25.Bxg7 Kxg7; 26.Rg1+ Black's king cannot

survive. **24.gxf7+ Kf8; 25.Be3.** Black's condition is critical, but Larsen comes up with a clever attempt to stay in the game.

**25...d5!** Larsen gives up a pawn to blunt White's bishop at b3. This was his best chance. **26.exd5.** 26.Bxd5? falls into the trap. 26...Rxc2; 27.Qxc2 Rxc2; 28.Kxc2 Qe2+; 29.Bd2 Bh6 and Black's h-pawn is more dangerous than the pawn at f7!

**26...Rxf7; 27.d6!** The discovered attack on the rook also sends White's passed pawn into the red zone, just two steps away from promotion, **27...Rf6; 28.Bg5.** The game is effectively over. Not only does Bobby get his exchange back, but with Black's forces occupied with the passed pawn, the king is a dead duck. **28... Qb7; 29.Bxf6 Bxf6; 30.d7 Rd8; 31.Qd6+.** 31.Qh6+ was more efficient, mating in three, but Larsen **resigned** anyway.

# WHEN ANY MOVE LOSES

## THE PLAYERS
Bobby Fischer (White)
vs.
Hector Rossetto (Argentina)

## THE LOCATION
The International Tournament,
in Mar del Plata, Argentina,
on 4/5/1959

### LESSON: ZUGZWANG

The German term "zugzwang" has no direct English translation. It generally refers to a position where a player loses because of the obligation to move. If a "pass" were possible, the game would not be lost. Chess does not allow a player to simply sit on the position. Some move must be made at each turn.

The zugzwang concept has a very important role in the endgame. Thousands of critical positions are wins for one side only because the other side is obliged to move. Often a zugzwang trick is the critical element in an endgame postion that may take dozens of moves to reach it.

A zugzwang position is often the last act in a game, as the player "in zugzwang" (or, less formally, "zugged") may as well resign, and usually does.

The zugzwang lies at the very end of the game, but there are plenty of exciting adventures on the way!

**1.e4 c5; 2.Nf3 e6; 3.d4 cxd4; 4.Nxd4 a6.**

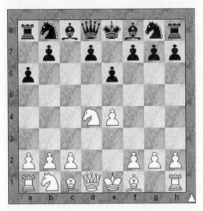

The Kan Variation is a flexible formation typical of the Sicilian Defense that is popular at all levels of play. The slightly weak dark squares can be patrolled by Black's bishop, queen and knights. The idea is to get in an early ...d5, usually after castling the king to safety. The opening can easily slide into other Sicilian types, including the Scheveningen, Classical, and Hedgehog formations.

**5.c4.** The Maroczy Bind formation by White, intended to prevent Black's "Sicilian break" with ...d5, is no longer considered particularly effective against the Kan. At the time, however, it was highly regarded. **5...Qc7?!** It is better to play ...Nf6 immediately and deal with the queen later. **6.Nc3 Nf6; 7.Bd3.** The bishop does not belong here and Fischer regretted the decision. Black's counterplay often involves moving the bishop to b4, so White should have advanced the pawn to a3 to prevent that. **7...Nc6; 8.Be3?** Bobby is playing the opening sloppily, which didn't happen often. If Rossetto had replied correctly, Black would have gained the upper hand right away. 8.Nxc6 dxc6; 9.O-O with equal chances was the best White could hope for at this point.

**8...Nxd4?!** The knight should move, but not capture. 8...Ne5! is correct, transferring the knight to the kingside. It threatens to jump to g4, where, if White is castled, there would be the threat of checkmate at h2. The knight isn't going to be exchanged for the bishop at d3, because that is White's "bad" bishop and the knight is far superior to it.

**9.Bxd4 Bc5.** Black's position doesn't look too bad, until you look a the bishop at c8 and think about its future. Eventually, it can sneak to c6 via d7, but that will take time. Even at an early age, Bobby appreciated the possibilities that come with extra moves. **10.Bc2.** 10.Bxc5 Qxc5 11.O-O d6 wouldn't have given Black any problems.

**10...d6; 11.O-O.** Castling is the obvious move, and no one seems to question the wisdom of the move. I think that the critical alternative of capturing at f6 deserves a look. 11.Bxf6 gxf6 shatters Black's kingside, though it does concede the bishop pair. White can change the situation by getting rid of a pair of bishops. 12.Ba4+ Bd7; 13.Bxd7+ Qxd7; 14.O-O, and unless Black can mount a serious attack on the g-file, White can eventually make good progress on the queenside. I prefer White's chances here to those in the game. **11...Bd7.**

**12.Na4.** Although Fischer didn't think that White had much of an advantage, even that is rather optimistic. Indeed, despite some inferior moves, Black had a chance to gain the upper hand. **12... Bxd4?** 12...Bxa4; 13.Bxa4+ Ke7! is recommended by Huebner, and it certainly seems as though Black has the better long term chances. A king in the center is not always vulnerable, though as a general rule such king moves are considered dangerous. White's pawns at c4 and e4 are weak. Black will play ...Rhd8 and then can walk the king to safety via f8.

**13.Qxd4 Rd8.** 13...e5 is possible here. The backward pawn at d6 will be offset by White's horrible bishop and weak pawns. Eventually the White knight can get to d5, but, after an exchange, Black is heading for an endgame with a much more mobile bishop.

Huebner analyzed this plan to a likely draw. **14.Rfd1 O-O!** Black offers the d-pawn as a temporary sacrifice. Fischer is wise to decline. If White captures at d6, then Black exchanges queens, captures the knight at a4 and then the pawn at e4. The bishop at c2 is overworked, having to defend both a4 and e4.

**15.Rac1!** It is often useful to aim your rook against an enemy king or queen, regardless of how much junk lies on the path. At some point, the interfering pieces may be removed, and tactics will arise. For example, if White removes both central pawns, Bxh7+ would win the Black queen by discovered attack. This clever move discouraged Black from risking ...b5, which would allow the c-pawn to get out of the way. 15.Qxd6 Qxd6; 16.Rxd6 Bxa4; 17.Rxd8 Rxd8; 18.Bxa4 Nxe4 would get the pawn back with an even endgame.

**15...Qa5.** Just as it was wise for White to aim the rook at the queen, it is equally wise for the queen to get out of the way. She supports the attack on the knight at a4, and can transfer to the center or kingside as needed. **16.Qb6.** Fischer offers an exchange of queens. It is rare for young players to want to enter tricky endgames against experienced opponents, but Bobby had correctly evaluated the endgame as being in his favor. **16...Qxb6?** This is a poor decision.

Fischer was correct to assess the transfer of the queen to e5 as dubious, but the game could have taken a rather exciting turn if she headed to the kingside. 16...Qg5!? would have offered Black a choice of pawns at d6 or b7. But there was a hidden price! Now 17.Qxd6? is a trick that backfires. 17...Bxa4; 18.Qxd8 Rxd8; 19.Rxd8+ Be8. But 17.Rxd6? drops a rook to 17...Qxc1+! On the other hand, 17.Qxb7 runs into 17...Bxa4; 18.Bxa4 Rb8;

19.Qxa6 Rxb2; 20.Rc2 Rbb8, which would have provided enough compensation for a pawn. White's bishop is useless, and the pawn at e4 is under attack. Black can always handle the queenside pawns by planting the knight at c5.

**17.Nxb6 Bc6; 18.f3 Nd7!** It is this move that convinced Rossetto to enter the endgame. If knights are exchanged Black can just manage to hold the position by doubling rooks on the d-file and bringing the king over to help. White's bad bishop makes it impossible to gain any advantage.

**19.Nd5!** This probably came as a shock. The point is that if Black captures the knight with the e-pawn, then after White recaptures with the e-pawn, there is no escape for the bishop. Rossetto knew better than to fall for that, but was too concerned about the possibility of Fischer using the knight to give a check at e7, followed by a capture at c6. So he got rid of the knight by taking it with his bishop.

**19...Bxd5?** A bad decision. 19...Ne5!; 20.Ne7+ Kh8; 21.Nxc6 bxc6 was best. Perhaps Rossetto didn't see that on 22.Ba4 he could establish the knight outpost at e5 by playing 22...g5! Fischer pointed out that Black could then march the king along the dark squares to e7, with a fully satisfactory position.

**20.exd5 e5.** Fischer wrote that 20…Ne5 was safer. He would have played 21.Be4, expecting Black to play 21…b6 where White has no real advantage because the bishop is so limited in scope.

**21.b4.** The c5 square is not only made unavailable to the Black knight. Fischer intends to occupy the square with one of his own pawns! **21…g6; 22.Ba4 b6; 23.Rd3.** White doesn't have any significant advantage, but the Black position is not easy to play. When Rossetto played …g6, the idea was to get ready for …f5, at least taking some kingside initiative. This plan is not bad, but has to be properly timed.

**23…f5?** This was premature. There were queenside issues that had to be dealt with. The proper strategy here was to keep White from carrying out the intended advance to c5. The weak link in White's position is the pawn at g4, so it should have been challenged right away. 23…a5! 24.a3 f5 was the correct plan, according to Fischer, who didn't see any path to a win.

**24.Ra3!** An odd position for the rook, but it completely eliminates counterplay on the a-file, and threatens to eat a pawn after capturing the knight. **24…Nb8.** This deals with the immediate problem, but now the superiority of the bishop over the knight is obvious. The knight was hoping to get to c5. That's not going to happen. **25.c5!** The decisive operation begins! The queenside is smashed open, and the bishop becomes even more powerful.

**25...bxc5; 26.bxc5 dxc5; 27.Rxc5.** The passed pawn and White's active pieces will quickly overwhelm Black's position. The game is not yet hopeless, but Black is up against the wall. **27...Kg7; 28.Rb3 Rf7; 29.d6 Nd7; 30.Rc7.**

The invasion of the seventh rank will soon see both rooks combine their power. Enemy doubled rooks on the seventh rank are usually the prelude to a funeral march for the king. **30...Nf8; 31.Rbb7 Rxc7; 32.dxc7!** The pawn is just one square from promotion. Better yet, that square is a light square, which can be easily attacked by the bishop.

**32...Rc8; 33.Bb3!** This keeps the Black king penned in. There are several ways of winning, but Fischer chooses the most elegant. He will place Black in zugzwang. In zugzwang, any move by the zugzwanged side loses, since the rules allowed a "pass." **33...a5.** 33...Kf6 loses immediately to 34.Rb8!

**34.a4 h6; 35.h3 g5; 36.g4 fxg4; 37.hxg4.** Black **resigned.**

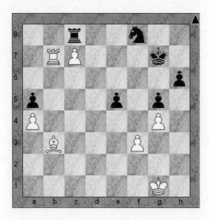

The zugzwang cannot be escaped. If Black moves the rook, or the king, then Rb8 wins. If the knight moves from f8, the bishop will get to e6. Black could play suicide pawn moves to e4 and h5, but that still only postpones the inevitable.

## GAME #5

# FAILING THE ENDGAME EXAM

**THE PLAYERS**
Bobby Fischer (White)
vs.
Paul Keres (Soviet Union)

**THE LOCATION**
The International Grandmaster Tournament, in Zurich, Switzerland, on 10/1/1959

## LESSON: IMPORTANCE OF THE ENDGAME

When you start playing chess most games end decisively because players tend to make some bad mistakes. As you get better, you find it's not so easy to win with knockout punches or simply by winning a piece or two and then going into endgame with one or more extra queens.

When you reach the level where players don't just leave pieces hanging around to be captured, you need to learn as much as you can about chess endgames. The endgame begins when enough pieces have been removed from the board that a direct attack is no longer likely to succeed. Some people think that the endgame begins when queens are no longer on the board, but that's not true. There are many endgames involving queens and some other pieces. There isn't a precise dividing line between the middle game and the endgame. Once you reach the endgame, however, an entirely different set of skills is required.

In the endgame, you need to know which small advantages can be converted into a winning position, and which ones will lead to a joint conclusion if your opponent has sufficient scale. Bobby Fischer was a particularly strong endgame player and so it is very instructive to see how he converts a small advantage into an important victory.

**1.e4 e5; 2.Nf3 Nc6; 3.Bb5 a6; 4.Ba4 Nf6; 5.O-O Be7; 6.Re1 b5; 7.Bb3 O-O; 8.c3 d6; 9.h3 Na5.**

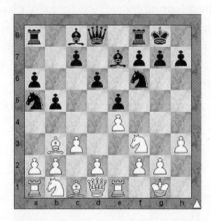

For many, many years this was the main line of the Spanish Game (Ruy Lopez). In modern play, 9…Re8 has eclipsed this move, and there are many alternatives. When this game was played, however, Mikhail Chigorin's ancient plan 9…Na5 was the focus of attention. After nine moves by each side, White is still quite some distance from full development. This allows Black to actively contest the battle for the center. Still, White has good control of many important light squares.

**10.Bc2.** Naturally, White preserves the light square bishop. Black's knight will eventually retreat to c6, but first the pawn will advance to c5, keeping pressure on the d4-square. **10...c5; 11.d4 Qc7.** This is a nice, safe square for the queen. White is not likely to get a knight to d5 in the near future, and there is no other way to attack the queen. **12.Nbd2 cxd4.** 12…Bd7; 13.Nf1 Rfe8; 14.Ne3 g6; 15.dxe5 dxe5; 16.Nh2 Rad8; 17.Qf3 was the way Fischer's game against Unzicker went in round 8. He won that one, too.

**13.cxd4 Bb7.** 13…Nc6; 14.Nb3 Bb7; 15.d5 Na5; 16.Nxa5 Qxa5; 17.a4 had given White a good game in Larsen vs. Keres, from round 9. **14.Nf1.** Fischer sticks with the traditional plan of transferring the knight to the kingside. Usually it heads for f5, especially when Black has removed the bishop from the c8-h3 diagonal. 14.d5 closes up the center. This is known as the Panov Attack. Fischer prefers to keep the position fluid.

**14...Rac8.** This is generally considered the best of Black's many options. Certainly Black wants a rook on the c-file, and the other rook can be used in the center. **15.Bd3.** The bishop sits here until the rook can slide over to c1, after which it can retreat to a comfortable position at b1. **15...Nc6.** This move was criticized at the time, but it is now considered fully respectable. 15...d5!? is an interesting alternative which leads to a messy center. Black usually manages to equalize as the central pawns leave the board.

**16.Ne3 Rfe8; 17.Nf5.** This is consistent with White's usual plan, though advancing the pawn to d5 first is considered more promising. The knight takes up a wonderful outpost. Black is more or less obliged to retreat the bishop to f8 to prevent it from being captured and to lend support to g7. White will move more forces into position to attack the kingside. Black's counterplay lies on the c-file and in the center.

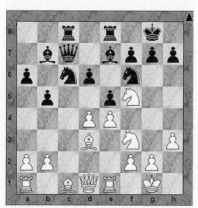

**17...Bf8; 18.Bg5 Nd7.** If the knight goes, so does the king's protection. So black has to hang on to the knight. **19.Rc1.** It is often useful to aim a rook at the enemy queen, Here the immediate threat is d5, winning the Black knight at c6, which is pinned. **19...Qb8.** Black wisely unpins. **20.Bb1.** A useful move, since the bishop

is just as effective from b1, and now the c-file can be controlled.
**20...Nxd4; 21.N3xd4.**

**21...Rxc1?** A tempting intermezzo, but Keres should just have
captured the knight at d4. He didn't realize that the retreat of the
bishop from g5, to capture the rook, actually aids White's attack,
as you'll see. 21...exd4; 22.Rxc8 Qxc8; 23.Qxd4 Nc5 would have
been just a little better for White.

**22.Bxc1 exd4.** Keres expected Fischer to grab the weakling at
d4, but failed to sense the danger on the kingside. Black's king has
just the pawn barrier and the bishop for defense. It seems that is
enough, since White has only a knight in attacking position. Fischer
launches a blistering attack anyway!

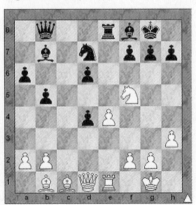

**23.Nh6+! gxh6.** Black must accept, or drop the f-pawn for nothing. **24.Qg4+.** This would not be available had Black not exchanged rooks at c1. The double attack on king and knight gets the piece back, and Black's position is a mess. **24...Kh8; 25.Qxd7 Bd5.** Black takes advantage of the pin on the e-pawn. If White captures at d5, the rook at e1 falls. **26.Qf5 Re5; 27.Qf3.** Black's pawns are a mess, but he does have an extra one and the pieces, except the bishop at f8, are fairly mobile. Fischer needs to be careful to find the precise move and exploit the small advantage.

**27...f5.** This is a bold attempt at counterplay. The pressure at e4 is intense, but Fischer sacrifices the pawn for an attack. **28.Bf4! Re8; 29.Qh5!** A strong move, though there is nothing wrong with 29.Qd1, targeting the weak pawn at d4 while breaking the pin on the e-pawn. **29...Bxe4.** Black must use the bishop, because if the rook captures it would fall to White's bishop at b1, and if the pawn is used, then the bishop will be captured by White's queen. **30.f3 Bc6; 31.Rc1!** The rook gets out of trouble on the e-file and takes up a position on the open c-file, attacking the bishop. **31...Bd7.**

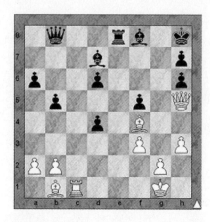

**32.Bxh6!** White had the choice between this pawn and the one at f5. It may seem strange to go after the weak doubled pawn, but the idea is to eliminate Black's dark square bishop, leaving the king more vulnerable. **32...Re6!** A nice defense. When White captures at f8, Black will recapture with the queen, so that all three of his pieces will be in a position to help with the defense. **33.Bxf8 Qxf8; 34.Qh4!** Fischer precisely calculates that the endgame is favorable, but Keres has no choice but to defend the weak pawn at d4, allowing an exchange of queens. **34...Qf6; 35.Qxf6+ Rxf6; 36.Kf2.**

This move has a slight blemish. Seizing the seventh rank immediately with the rook might have been more efficient. Seizing the seventh rank and centralizing the king are of equal importance, but the move order chosen by Fischer gives Black a chance to bring the king into the game and set up an alternative defense. In general, a forcing move is the right choice because it limits the opponent's options. Notice that Fischer doesn't bother going after the pawn at d4 with the rook. It isn't going anywhere. 36.Rc7 Rf7; 37.Ra7 Be6; 38.Rxa6 Rc7; 39.Kf2 Rc1; 40.Bd3 is Fischer's analysis. He pointed out that Black's pawns would be "hopelessly weak."

**36...Kg7; 37.Rc7 Rf7; 38.Ke2 f4?!** Keres should not have given up his control of e4. Placing the pawns on dark squares makes them harder to defend, when your only bishop patrols the light squares.

38...Kf6!; 39.Ra7 Bc8? (39...Rg7 would have provided more counterplay.) 40.Rxf7+ Kxf7 was evaluated by Fischer as equal.

**39.Ra7.** 39.Kd3? Bf5+ was the trap Keres hoped to spring, but Fischer doesn't fall for such stuff. **39...Kf6 40.Rxa6 Re7+.**

Time control has been reached. The endgame is complicated, and each side had the advantage of adjournment analysis to try to work it out. And back then, there were no computers to assist!

**41.Kf2.** 41.Kd2 is bad because of 41...Rg7! The king must keep an eye on the g-pawn. **41...Be6!?** A very good defensive plan. In some endgames it is worthwhile to sacrifice a pawn or two just to get the pieces into active positions. Black doesn't really have any use for the pawn at d6, anyway.

However, Huebner points out that Black might have done better to move the bishop to f5. In the cold light of analysis, one can double-check everything to make sure that the exchange of bishops and loss of the d-pawn can be defended. Most chessplayers will hesitate to trade pieces unless they are quite sure the simplified endgame is safe. I do not know which move was sealed in the adjournment envelope. If it was not Bobby's 41st move, then one can well understand how an exhausted player would choose a less radical move. Better to contemplate the exchange of bishops after dinner, than to try to work it all out at the board. **42.Rxd6 Ke5.**

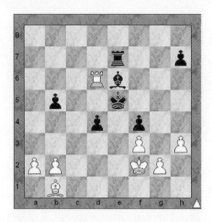

**43.Rc6.** 43.Rb6 Bc4; 44.b3 allows 44...d3!; 45.bxc4 bxc4 where Fischer believed the connected passed pawns would hold the draw. Since that isn't immediately obvious, consider the following line. 46.a4 Kd4; 47.a5 Re2+; 48.Kf1 Re3! (Or 48...Re5 49.a6 c3 50.Rd6+!) 49.Rd6+ Kc3 50.Ba2 50...Re2! 51.Bxc4 Kxc4 52.a6 Ra2 and the game should indeed end in a draw. It could be worse. Pushing the passed pawn with 50.a6? is a less pleasant experience after 50...d2; 51.a7 Rd3!; 52.Rxd3+ cxd3; 53.a8=Q d1=Q+; 54.Kf2 Qxb1 and White is fighting for a draw.

**43...Bd5; 44.Rh6!** The rook drives the enemy king back. **44... Rc7; 45.Rh5+.** 45.Rb6 Rc1; 46.Bxh7? Bc4 threatens the embarrassing 47...Rf1 mate! **45...Kd6; 46.Rh6+ Ke5; 47.Rh5+ Kd6.** Fischer didn't want to continue to repeat the position and concede a draw, but he fails to find the best path to the win.

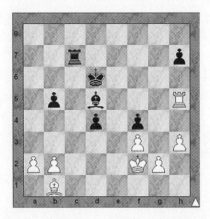

**48.Rf5?** 48.b3! was correct. 48...Rc1; 49.Be4 Bxe4; 50.fxe4 leaves Black with no good defense. The king and pawn endgame after 50...Rc5; 51.Rxc5 Kxc5; 52.a4 is an easy win.

**48...Rc1; 49.Bd3 Rd1.** 49...Bc4? would have been refuted in fine fashion by 50.Rxf4! Bxd3; 51.Rxd4+ Kc5; 52.Rxd3 Rc2+; 53.Kg3 Rxb2; 54.Ra3 and White wins.

**50.Ke2 Rg1; 51.Kf2 Rd1; 52.Ke2 Rg1.** These little repetitive episodes were played to gain a little time on the clock. **53.Rg5.**

**53...Bxa2?** The exchange of pawns turns out to be a mistake. 53...Ra1 was an easy draw, according to Keres. But he didn't spot it during the game. 54.Bxh7 Bc4+; 55.Kd2 Rxa2; 56.Kc2 Ra1 would have provided enough counterplay, according to Keres. White has an extra pawn, but Black's d-pawn is advanced. So let's look a little further. 57.Bd3! Ra2. Black threatens to swap bishops and win the b-pawn, while protecting the pawn at b5. 58.h4! Bxd3+; 59.Kxd3 Rxb2; 60.h5 Rb1. The rook moves into defensive formation behind the h-pawn. That's the best defense. Retreating to the back rank isn't as good, because White can advance the pawn to h7 and play Rf8. After 61.Kxd4 b4; 62.Rg6+ Ke7; 63.h6 b3; 64.Rb6! Kf7; 65.Ke4 b2; 66.Kxf4 Rh1; 67.Rxb2 Rxh6; 68.Rb7+ White wins easily. No better is 64...Rh1; 65.h7! Kf7; 66.Rxb3 Rxh7; 67.Rb7+ Kg6; 68.Rxh7 Kxh7; 69.Ke4 etc.

**54.Bxb5 Rb1; 55.Kd3.** The position is still complicated, and the players had a few moves to go before it could be adjourned again, leaving time for overnight analysis. Black failed to appreciate the potential of the b1-h7 diagonal. Fair enough, since Black has a rook at b1. But if the rook is gone, then the bishop can make good use of the square.

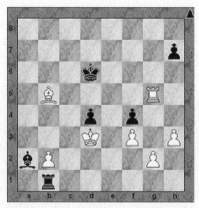

**55...h6?** 55...Rxb2!; 56.Ke4 Bb1+! was correct, and it "should hold the draw," according to Fischer. 57.Bd3 Re2+! (57...Bxd3+; 58.Kxd3 Rb4; 59.Rh5 leaves Black with too many weaknesses.) 58.Kxd4 Rd2. This doesn't win the bishop, because White can defend it. However, the price is the loss of the g-pawn. 59.Rd5+ Ke6; 60.Ke4 Bxd3+; 61.Rxd3 Rxg2; 62.Kxf4 Kf6 is not winnable if Black defends correctly.

**56.Rh5 Rxb2; 57.Kxd4 Rxg2; 58.Rxh6+.**

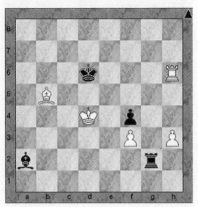

Here the game was adjourned again. Both sides worked overnight, studying the position in detail. **58...Ke7; 59.Ke4 Rg5; 60.Ba6?**

Fischer's analysis was flawed. He knew that he couldn't swap bishops without running into an endgame known to be drawn, even though White would have two pawns and Black would lose the remaining pawn. It is very important to know the many drawing tricks in rook endgames! He also had to keep the rooks on the board, unless he could prevent Black from using the well known trick of sacrificing the bishop for the f-pawn and retreating the king to h8. 60.Bd3 Bf7; 61.Kxf4 Rh5 would have led to a draw. 62.Rxh5 Bxh5; 63.Bf5 allows Black to escape with 63...Bxf3!; 64.Kxf3 Kf6; 65.Kf4 Kg7; 66.Kg5 Kh8 with the famous "wrong bishop" endgame. The Black king cannot be forced out of the corner. 60.Bf1! Rg1; 61.Ba6! would have been the right plan.

**60...Bf7?** Keres had actually seen the correct defense in his analysis, but when he was back at the board he forgot what he had studied. Adjournment analysis was a lot like cramming for an exam. A tremendous amount of material is reviewed, but it won't all stick. This one bad move cost him the game. 60...Bb1+! gives up the f-pawn, which can't be saved anyway. But it lets Black regroup and exchange rooks, leading to the known draw. 61.Kxf4 Rf5+; 62.Kg4 Rf6!; 63.Rxf6 Kxf6 brings Black's king into a perfect position. He can run to h8 after the bishop is eventually sacrificed for the f-pawn. The control of the b1-h7 diagonal insures that Black's plan cannot fail.

**61.Bc8!** Fischer has just enough time to bring his bishop to g4. **61...Rg6.** 61...Rc5; 62.Bg4 Rc4+; 63.Ke5 Ra4; 64.h4 Kf8; 65.Rb6 Rc4; 66.h5 wins, because 66...Bxh5?; 67.Bxh5 Rc5+ loses to 68.Kf6! Rxh5; 69.Rb8. Checkmate.

**62.Rh7 Kf8; 63.Bg4 Rg7.** Fischer has just one more trap to avoid. An exchange of rooks on this move would lead to the drawing lines. 63...Rxg4 is a trick that backfires on Black. 64.Rxf7+ Kxf7; 65.hxg4 and White will prevail. 63...Rb6; 64.Kxf4 Kg8 was claimed to be a draw by Barcza, in the tournament book. Fischer didn't mention the line. Let's have a look. 65.Rh4 Rb4+; 66.Kg5 Rb5+; 67.Bf5 Be6; 68.Rf4 Kg7; 69.h4 Bxf5; 70.Rxf5 Rb1 is a defensible rook endgame. 66.Kg3 is a better try, but 66...Kg7 might work, because the bishop is pinned. 67.Bd7 Rxh4; 68.Kxh4 Kf6 gives Black the appropriate defensive formation.

**64.Rh6!** 64.Rxg7? Kxg7; 65.Kxf4 Kf6. The bishop will be sacrificed for the f-pawn, eventually reaching the draw we've already seen.

**64...Rg6.** Black has nothing better, but now the exchange does work, because Black's king can't get to f6, which is necessary for the defense against White's pawns. **65.Rxg6! Bxg6+; 66.Kxf4 Kg7;**

**67.Kg5 Bd3; 68.f4 Be4; 69.h4 Bd3; 70.h5 Be4; 71.h6+ Kh8; 72.Bf5!** The enemy bishop is forced off the key diagonal. This plan isn't available when Black's king occupies f6. 72.f5? would be a big error because 72…Bxf5! leads to a draw.

**72…Bd5; 73.Bg6 Be6.** Still trying to prevent the f-pawn from advancing. **74.Kf6 Bc4; 75.Kg5 Be6; 76.Bh5 Kh7; 77.Bg4!** It took Fischer a few moves to come up with the right plan. During the adjournment analysis, he probably stopped when he reached a position where his king controlled f6, leaving the final bits as an elementary problem to be solved at the board.

**77…Bc4.** 77…Bxg4; 78.Kxg4 Kxh6 is a lost King and Pawn endgame. 79.Kf5 Kg7; 80.Ke6 Kf8; 81.Kf6 Ke8; 82.Kg7 Ke7; 83.f5 etc. **78.f5 Bf7; 79.Bh5 Bc4.** Black obviously can't afford to exchange. **80.Bg6+ Kg8; 81.f6.** Keres **resigned.**

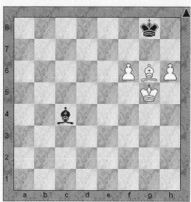

It may still be unclear that Black is lost. After all, can't Black sacrifice the bishop when the pawn reaches f7? In fact, it takes a few moves, but White will be able to promote a pawn. 81…Bb3; 82.Kf4 Kh8; 83.Ke5 Bc4; 84.Kd6 Bb3; 85.Ke7 Bc4; 86.Bf7 Bd3; 87.Be8! Bc4; 88.Bd7 Bg8; 89.Be6 Bh7; 90.f7 is the solution given by Fischer himself. The finish is 90…Bg6; 91.f8=Q+ Kh7; 92.Qg7. Checkmate.

# GAME #6

# A LITTLE PAWN DECIDES THE GAME

**THE PLAYERS**
Bobby Fischer (White)
vs.
Max Euwe (Holland)

**THE LOCATION**
The Olympiad,
in Leipzig, Germany,
on 11/3/1960

## LESSON: CREATING A NEW QUEEN FROM A PASSED PAWN

One of the most common winning methods in the endgame is to advance one of your pawns all the way to the other side of the board where it can be promoted to a queen or any other piece, except for a King or pawn.

The easiest pawn to advance is a passed pawn. A passed pawn is one that has no enemy pawns either blocking the path directly in front of it, or on adjacent files in a position to capture the pawn, should it advance to a protected square. Such pawns may be able to advance easily, but they can also be quite vulnerable to attack. Knowing whether a passed pawn is weak or strong is a fine art that requires considerable practice and experience.

If you have a passed pawn, even if it is an extra pawn, it isn't easy to promote it. You need to keep your pawn protected, often using a rook behind it, and also to clear the squares in front of the pawn so that it can advance. Endgames with passed pawns are among the first you should study if you want to improve your results in this most difficult stage of the game.

1.e4 c6; 2.d4 d5; 3.exd5 cxd5; 4.c4 Nf6; 5.Nc3 Nc6; 6.Nf3.

The Panov Attack is one of White's most popular strategies against the Caro-Kann Defense. White develops quickly and enjoys a small advantage in space. It may be necessary to accept an isolated pawn, but isolated pawns are no longer considered to be a disadvantage if they are well-supported d-pawns.

**6...Bg4.** This is Black's most aggressive plan. It leads to endgame positions with a shattered White kingside, but White gets the bishop pair. **7.cxd5 Nxd5; 8.Qb3.** White attacks the light squares left vulnerable by the departure of the bishop for the kingside. Black responds by capturing the knight and inflicting serious damage on the kingside.

**8...Bxf3; 9.gxf3 e6.** This well known temporary sacrifice of the b-pawn has long been the main line of the Endgame Variation of the Panov. **10.Qxb7 Nxd4; 11.Bb5+ Nxb5; 12.Qc6+.** White throws in this check to inconvenience the Black king before capturing the knight. **12...Ke7; 13.Qxb5.**

This position has been reached at least 500 times, and it is now established that Black should play 13...Qd7 right away. The exchange of knights, seen here, lost a lot of popularity as a result of this game.

**13...Nxc3; 14.bxc3 Qd7; 15.Rb1!** This was Bobby's prepared new move, and ever since this game Black has had a terrible time in the variation. The open b-file will play an important role all the way to the end of the game. **15...Rd8?** Although this is a somewhat obvious try, threatening checkmate at d1, it does not begin to solve Black's problems. Objectively, Black should try 15...Rc8, targeting the weak pawn at c3. **16.Be3 Qxb5; 17.Rxb5 Rd7.**

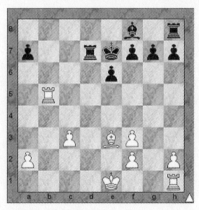

We have reached an endgame where, despite White's shattered pawn structure, the passed c-pawn and more active pieces give

White a serious advantage. White can pick off the a-pawn whenever he wants to.

**18.Ke2!** Bobby activates the other rook. **18...f6; 19.Rd1!** Black's only active rook is invited to leave the game, but there isn't an acceptable alternative for Black. **19...Rxd1; 20.Kxd1 Kd7; 21.Rb8.** Threatening to exploit the pin with Bc5, so Black's reply is pretty much forced. **21...Kc6; 22.Bxa7 g5; 23.a4 Bg7.**

**24.Rb6+!** Bobby correctly declines the invitation to exchange rooks. Then the win would be tricky, despite the passed pawns, because the bishop is of the "wrong color". It can't chase a king from a8 or c8. 24.Rxh8 Bxh8; 25.Bd4 e5; 26.Be3 Bg7 isn't easy, for example 27.Kc2 Bf8; 28.Kb3 Bd6; 29.a5 e4!; 30.fxe4 Bxh2; 31.a6 h5; 32.a7 Kb7 is more likely to be won by Black, than White!

**24...Kd5; 25.Rb7 Bf8.** Black just can't get the rook into the game. **26.Rb8 Bg7; 27.Rb5+ Kc6; 28.Rb6+ Kd5; 29.a5.** Fischer has cut the enemy king off on the 6th rank and threatens simply Bb8 and a6-a7-a8. **29...f5; 30.Bb8 Rc8; 31.a6.** The weak pawn at c3 is no longer significant. **31...Rxc3; 32.Rb5+.**

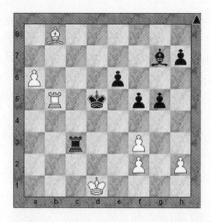

**32...Kc4.** 32...Kc6 was suggested by Reuben Fine, who showed it to Bobby after the game. 33.Ra5 Bd4 was the idea, and Bobby reacted with 34.Be5?, then Fine revealed the stunner 34...Rc5! where the game should be drawn, though it is White facing the uphill battle. 34.a7 Bxa7; 35.Rxa7 Rxf3; 36.Rxh7 Rxf2 holds no winning chances for White. Fischer looked at the position again, and determined that 34.Ke2 would win.

**33.Rb7! Bd4; 34.Rc7+.** After the rooks come off, the endgame is an easy win for White. **34...Kd3; 35.Rxc3+ Kxc3; 36.Be5.** Black **resigned.**

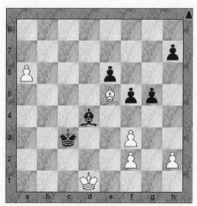

The pawn will get to a7 and then promote at a8. The bishop at d5 is pinned, and the capture of White's bishop at e5 wouldn't make any difference.

# GAME #7

# FIRING WITH BOTH BARRELS

**THE PLAYERS**
Bobby Fischer (White)
vs.
Samuel Reshevsky (U.S.A.)

**THE LOCATION**
The Match,
in New York, U.S.A.,
on 7/18/1961

## LESSON: USING OPEN FILES TO ATTACK

Most of the time, in order to attack successfully you need to use heavy artillery. The queen and rooks must participate if you need to demolish a solid defensive position. Since heavy artillery works best from a distance, weapons need straight lines aiming at the enemy target squares.

When there are no pawns on a file, it is referred to as an "open file." Informally, the same term is used when we talk about files that have only an enemy pawn on them because you can use your rooks or queen on the same line attacking from the front or the rear. Technically, that's a half-open or semi-open file.

In general, rooks belong on open files. They are usually moved to files that have already lost their pawns. It is very rare that a rook can remain on his home square and be certain of obtaining an open file later, though this does sometimes happen when the pawn in front of the rook marches forward to attack an enemy position and is eventually lost in the process.

Such cases can be seen in many variations of the Sicilian Defense, because the kings are usually castled on opposite flanks. This means that the rook pawns can be advanced on the flank against the enemy king, without exposing your own king to attack.

**1.e4 c5; 2.Nf3 Nc6; 3.d4 cxd4; 4.Nxd4 g6; 5.Nc3.** White can establish the once-dreaded "Maroczy Bind" here with 5.c4, but Fischer was quite content to let the game flow into the path of the Dragon Sicilian. During a later game in the match he adopted Maroczy's approach. **5...Bg7; 6.Be3 Nf6; 7.Be2.**

The advantage of Reshevsky's order of moves is that Fischer's favorite Yugoslav Attack, seen in the game against Larsen, is not available. If White tries that formation, eventually Black plays ...d5 in one move, without having the pawn step to d6 first. That gain of time is sufficient to achieve a fully equal game. So Bobby switches to the Classical Variation, which usually involves straightforward development and kingside castling.

**7...O-O; 8.f4 d6; 9.Nb3 Be6.** This is the normal post for the bishop, though it will come under attack by the White f-pawn at some point. Fischer was pleased to see this move, as he considered it inferior to launching a queenside attack with 9...a5. **10.g4 d5.** It is a bit odd to see this advance so soon after Black has played ...d6. It is the thematic "Sicilian break" where Black challenges White's central pawn.

**11.f5.** Fischer chooses the thematic advance of the f-pawn, driving back the enemy bishop. 11.exd5? Nxd5; 12.Nxd5 Qxd5; 13.Qxd5 Bxd5 would clearly demonstrate the superiority of Black's bishops, aiming at h1 and b2. **11...Bc8; 12.exd5.** White temporarily wins a pawn, but can't hold on to it. The real effect is to keep Black occupied with regaining the material, all the while laying the foundation of a kingside attack.

**12...Nb4; 13.Bf3.** Fischer holds on to the powerful pawn at d5, and lets the kingside pawns go. This opens more lines for a future attack against the enemy king. **13...gxf5; 14.a3! fxg4.** Black offers the knight in exchange for the powerful bishop at f3, but Bobby isn't buying! **15.Bg2!** Now Black's bishop is forced back to a6, where it is a long way from the kingside.

**15...Na6; 16.Qd3!** This move was part of Fischer's preparation for the game. It was discovered by the Soviet player Nei, and was already well known. **16...e6.** Fischer considered this the best defense, but it has been consigned to the dustbin of history and replaced by more effective plans. 16...Qd6; 17.O-O-O Nh5; 18.h3 Nf4 is a more promising defense.

**17.O-O-O.** Given the kingside situation, it is clear that the White king must seek shelter on the queenside. **17...Nxd5.** 17...exd5; 18.h3 must be met by 18...g3 , keeping the lines closed. 19.Bd4 is then very strong, with a discovered attack against the pawn at g3.

**18.h3 g3; 19.Rhg1.** Since the h-file remains closed, White shifts the rook to the g-file. Eventually the weak pawn at g3 must fall. Black's problem is a total lack of counterplay.

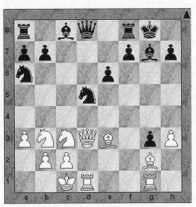

**19...Qd6?!** The queen defends the g-pawn but is herself vulnerable to attack. Bobby praises this move but there was a better way to defend the g-pawn, as pointed out by Huebner. 19...Qh4! has the advantage of both defending the pawn and covering key squares on the kingside and along the 4th rank.

**20.Bxd5 exd5; 21.Nxd5?** Grabbing the weak pawn right away was a mistake. The pawn isn't doing anything but taking up space, and Fischer later remarked that he should have played Bd4, to get rid of Black's most powerful defender. Black would then have had no meaningful defensive resources and the kingside would soon fall apart.

**21...Kh8!** Black gets away from g8, which is exposed on the g-file and also subject to attack by the knight, moving to f6 or e7. **22.Bf4.** This is the correct destination for the bishop. 22.Bd4 Bxd4; 23.Qxd4+ f6 doesn't achieve anything for White now.

**22...Qg6.** The queen can sit here more comfortably with the king evacuated to the h-file. At least now there are no potential pins. **23.Qd2 Bxh3!** Under time pressure, Reshevsky grabs the pawn without hesitation. Even though it opens up the h-file, the bishop will be able to work as a blockader of the g-file. It will be taking up a position at g4, where it can be supported by the h-pawn. **24.Rxg3 Bg4; 25.Rh1 Rfe8.** As White's rooks target the kingside, Black tries to gains some counterplay on the central files. **26.Ne3.** The pressure builds. Here, in time trouble, Reshevsky overlooked the only workable defense.

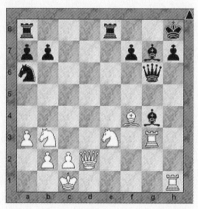

**26...Qe4?** 26...f5! was correct. Then if 27.Qh2 Black's king could just slide back to the g-file, according to Fischer's notes. 27...Kg8; 28.Qg2 still shows great promise for White, but some work lies ahead.

**27.Qh2 Be6.** There is nothing better. 27...Qxf4? runs into 28.Qxh7. Checkmate; 27...Bf5 allows the elegant 28.Rxg7! Kxg7; 29.Nxf5+ Qxf5; 30.Nd4 followed by Rg1.

**28.Rxg7!?** The exchange sacrifice brings a swift end to the game. Fischer had no problem investing a little material. After all, Black's knight and rooks just lay around uselessly taking up space. White's forces are in position to wrap things up easily, and even the knight at b3 will have something to say. 28.Nd2 would have been much more efficient, but less artistic. The queen would have to sacrifice herself at h1 to avoid mate. **28...Kxg7; 29.Qh6+ Kg8; 30.Rg1+ Qg6; 31.Rxg6+ fxg6.**

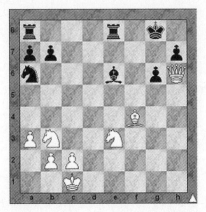

White has a material advantage, and the attack continues in full force. Black could resign with a clean conscience, but Reshevsky often battled on until his king was buried.

**32.Nd4 Rad8; 33.Be5 Rd7; 34.Nxe6 Rxe6; 35.Ng4 Rf7; 36.Qg5 Rf1+; 37.Kd2 h5; 38.Qd8+** Black **resigned.**

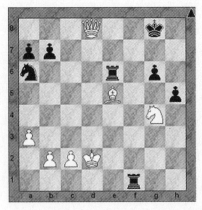

# GAME #8

# CASTLE OR DIE

**THE PLAYERS**
Bobby Fischer (White)
vs.
Mikhail Tal (Soviet Union)

**THE LOCATION**
The International Tournament,
in Bled, Slovenia,
on 9/4/1961

## LESSON: GET YOUR KING
## CASTLED OR PAY THE PRICE

Many pieces of chess wisdom are just generalization, not to be followed slavishly. Getting your king castled to safety, however, is almost always a good idea. It isn't merely one of the four goals of the opening. It is a maneuver that is often essential just to keep the king alive and breathing.

It is surprising how often this advice is ignored, with devastating results. This is even true of games at a professional level. Even when the players are grandmasters, or World Champions! Advanced players can afford to keep the king in the center for a while, in special circumstances. Beginners should attend to castling as the single most important part of their opening strategy.

Sometimes, castling is available but there is a better move to be found. Still, it is very rare that castling is an error with significant consequences. When in doubt, just do it!

**1.e4 c5; 2.Nf3 Nc6; 3.d4 cxd4; 4.Nxd4 e6; 5.Nc3 Qc7.**

Black adopts the Paulsen setup, a popular defense with a history that goes back well into the 19th century. The game can follow many different paths, but Bobby chooses a plan for White that limits Black's options.

**6.g3 Nf6?** Black's move is inaccurate. Though Fischer did not take up the challenge with 6.Nb5, he does so in the next move. It would have been wiser to play …a6 immediately, to prevent that plan.

**7.Ndb5 Qb8; 8.Bf4!** This is the point. Because White has a pawn at g3, this move is playable, and inconvenient for Black. **8…Ne5.**

Things are already pretty bad. Blocking with the pawn would have been even worse. 8…e5 would have been met by 9.Bg5 and then if 9…a6, White would play 10.Bxf6 gxf6; 11.Na3. Black then has to decide whether to part with the dark square bishop or play …b5, since a White knight at c4 would be very powerful.

**9.Be2.** White guards the weak f3 square while keeping an eye on c4. Since a bishop normally goes to g2 when the triangle of pawns is established, this may well have been overlooked by Tal. The simple threat is Qd4, with enormous pressure on the knight at e5. **9… Bc5.** The only move, really, since it prevents White from carrying out the plan and prepares to evacuate the king.

**10.Bxe5!** Fischer seizes the initiative and quickly establishes a dominating position. **10...Qxe5; 11.f4 Qb8; 12.e5!** Now if the knight retreats, White plays Ne4 and before long a knight will arrive at d6 with a permanent bind on Black's position. So Tal tries to counterattack and drive the enemy knight back.

**12...a6; 13.exf6!** No retreat for Bobby, who picks off a pawn on the next move. **13...axb5; 14.fxg7 Rg8; 15.Ne4 Be7.** The bishop retreats to guard the weak squares at d6 and f6. Black is not only a pawn down, but suffers from many pawn weaknesses and a horrible bishop at c8. **16.Qd4.** The queen takes up a powerful position in the center of the board. Normally, the queen has to work from the sides, because she can be vulnerable in the center. Black no longer has any knights, and the relevant files are closed to the rooks, so here she sits comfortably. **16...Ra4.** It is understandable that Tal wanted to go after the queen, but the rook is not well placed here and Fischer easily deflects the attack. So, as World Champion Botvinnik pointed out, it would have been better to move the queen away to c7. **17.Nf6+; Bxf6.** 17...Kd8?; 18.Qb6+ Qc7; 19.Qxc7+ Kxc7; 20.Nxg8 was clearly not an option.

**18.Qxf6 Qc7.** Here Bobby had to make a critical decision. It is time to get the king castled, since Black's pieces are coming to life on the queenside. Many players would immediately choose kingside castling, as the king would not be under immediate attack there. However, the advance of the f-pawn has weakened the kingside.

Fischer appreciated that despite the glare of the enemy rook and queen, his king would actually be much safer on the queenside, even if he has to give up the a-pawn!

**19.O-O-O! Rxa2; 20.Kb1.** The point is that b2 is defended by the queen at f6, and c2 can be handled by the bishop, which can move to d3. Then, if the bishop captures Black's h-pawn, the g-pawn may get promoted quickly. **20...Ra6.** 20...Qa5 is easily refuted by 21.b3! The White queen then covers all the squares on the a1-h8 diagonal.

**21.Bxb5?** This is clearly wrong, but as Bobby pointed out, he was intent on grabbing material so that he could finally defeat his rival. He should have gone for the jugular, instead of a pawn. 21.Bh5! would have been crushing. 21...d6; 22.Rhe1 Qe7; 23.Qh6 would have wrapped things up much more efficiently.

**21...Rb6; 22.Bd3 e5!?** Tal offers a pawn to release the pressure. This is an active defense. The discovered attack on the queen encourages White to capture at e5 with the queen, and then after the exchange of queens Black can try to grovel a draw in the endgame. Bobby had worked out a surprising reply.

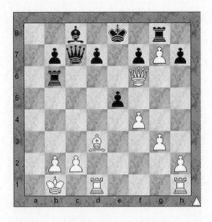

**23.fxe5!** A queen sacrifice! Bobby knew that he'd eventually win the other rook, so there was no real risk. Still, it was an elegant solution to the position. **23...Rxf6; 24.exf6 Qc5.** If the queen goes after the pawn at f6, Fischer would have defended the pawn with a rook. Black's bishop still hasn't moved, after two-dozen moves! There is no possibility of castling, and the rook on g8 has to stick around to prevent White's pawn from queening. In a less important game, Black might have considered resigning at this point! **25.Bxh7 Qg5; 26.Bxg8 Qxf6; 27.Rhf1 Qxg7; 28.Bxf7+ Kd8.** With two rooks and two connected passed pawns for the queen, there is no chance for survival. Tal, the "Magician," can't make like Houdini and escape his inevitable fate.

**29.Be6.** The pin, combined with the possibility of Rf7, picks off yet another pawn. **29...Qh6; 30.Bxd7 Bxd7; 31.Rf7 Qxh2; 32.Rdxd7+ Ke8; 33.Rde7+ Kd8; 34.Rd7+.** Fischer tosses in some checks just to make sure that time control is reached.

The result is a foregone conclusion, but is instructive in displaying some efficient technique. **34...Kc8; 35.Rc7+ Kd8; 36.Rfd7+ Ke8; 37.Rd1 b5; 38.Rb7 Qh5; 39.g4 Qh3; 40.g5 Qf3; 41.Re1+ Kf8; 42.Rxb5 Kg7; 43.Rb6 Qg3; 44.Rd1 Qc7; 45.Rdd6 Qc8; 46.b3 Kh7; 47.Ra6.** Finally, faced with checkmate or loss of the queen, Tal decided to **resign.**

# DEVELOP OR DIE

**THE PLAYERS**
Bobby Fischer (White)
vs.
Yefim Geller (Soviet Union)

**THE LOCATION**
The International Tournament,
in Bled, Slovenia,
on 9/10/1961

## LESSON: GET YOUR PIECES INTO POSITION TO DO BATTLE, OR YOUR KING WILL SUFFER

Castling isn't a complete prescription for the health of your king. Your army must take up positions to defend him, and attack the enemy at the same time. Key defenders usually include a knight, and it is useful to have a bishop in the neighborhood. Rooks and the queen aren't good defenders because they are too valuable.

So, the "minor pieces," as bishops and knights are known, must never be left in useless positions. Even if they can't help in an attack, they can be useful defenders.

Imagine that you have castled kingside as White. A knight can defend usefully from f3, or even f1! In either case, the h2-square is defended. At f3 the knight can leap into a kingside or central attack quickly, but it also can be attacked on that square. On f1, it isn't going to attack, but can't be easily dislodged.

Bishops are useful at g2, g3, and sometimes at f1 if the g2-pawn is under attack. In the first cases the bishops also attack, but at f1 it is safe. The balance between the natural desire to attack and the need to defend your king is a tricky one. It comes with experience.

**1.e4 e5; 2.Nf3 Nc6; 3.Bb5 a6; 4.Ba4.** Although Fischer was known for his contributions to the Exchange Variation (4.Bxc6) he was at least equally effective in the traditional main lines. **4...d6.** The Modern Steinitz Variation is an improvement on the strategy favored by the first World Champion who played 3...d6, because the bishop at a4 can be kicked back by ...b5 whenever Black wants to break the pin. **5.O-O Bg4; 6.h3!** Fischer challenges the bishop right away, forcing Black to make an important decision.

**6...Bh5.** Black can offer the bishop as a sacrifice by "defending" it with the h-pawn. If White captures, the rook at h8 stares menacingly at the White kingside.

6...h5!? sets a trap.

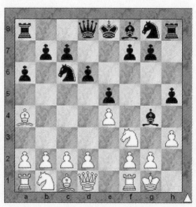

7.hxg4 hxg4; 8.Ne1? loses to 8...Qh4! Instead, White would play 7.d4 and the game might continue 7...b5; 8.Bb3 Nxd4. The bishop still exerts a lot of pressure because of the pin on the knight, and here White must capture. 9.hxg4 hxg4; 10.Ng5. The knight, protected by the bishop at c1, prevents the Black queen from getting to h4. Still, Black has two pawns for the piece. 10...Nh6 brings about an unclear position. The White knight cannot retreat to safety.

Returning to the game, White chose **7.c3.** This is a useful move that allows the bishop to retreat to c2, the natural home in the modern Spanish lines. In addition, the advance of a pawn to d4 has more support.

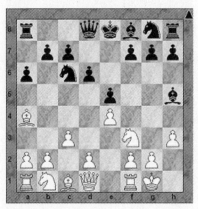

**7...Qf6?** This is not really a useful post for the queen, unless Black is committed to a strategy involving an exchange of the bishop for the knight at f3. Black should have placed his knight on this square instead, a far more natural plan. To be fair to the distinguished theoretician, Geller, it has to be said that Fischer had anticipated the opening and had spent some time developing a new gambit approach to the position.

**8.g4!** Fischer drives back the bishop, preventing the exchange at f3. Sure, the kingside gets a bit weak, but Black's king is still in the center, and the center files are about to be blasted open. Fischer will have to give up the e-pawn, but by removing the pawn, Geller's king will be exposed.

**8...Bg6; 9.d4!** Fischer commented that he felt that the "traffic jam" on the kingside would keep Black from developing, and that would compensate for the weakened kingside protection. **9...Bxe4.** Otherwise Fischer would have played Bg5 followed by d5 after the forced queen move to e6. Then White wins a full piece.

**10.Nbd2.** It is normal for this knight to temporarily block the bishop in the Spanish Game. White's position is so strong that only three games have been played from this position, all won by White. **10...Bg6.**

10...Bd3; 11.Bxc6+ bxc6; 12.Re1 O-O-O; 13.Re3 gave White a huge initiative in Smyslov vs. Medina, Tel Aviv Olympiad, 1964.

10...Bxf3; 11.Nxf3 e4; 12.Re1 d5; 13.c4 (13.Bg5 Qd6; 14.c4! is more convincing. The Black king is trapped in the center, and White threatens cxd5 followed by Bb3 and Rxe4.) 13...Bb4; 14.cxd5? (14. Re3! would have kept enough compensation for the pawn.) 14... Bxe1; 15.dxc6 Bxf2+; 16.Kxf2 b5; 17.Bb3 exf3; 18.Qxf3 O-O-O; 19.Qxf6 Nxf6 was eventually won by White in Hartston vs. Aijala, at Oerebro (Sweden) 1966, but the position is clearly in Black's favor.

**11.Bxc6+ bxc6.** Black's queenside barrier is destroyed, so the king cannot take shelter there.

**12.dxe5.** Fischer later thought that attacking the c-pawn directly would have been stronger, possibly crushing. But then he applied himself to the defense and found a remedy. 12.Qa4 Kd7! would have proven hard to crack. The king is probably safe there, even after the d-file is opened, because the bishop will be able to come to d6. 13.dxe5 dxe5; 14.Nc4 Bd6 is the line Fischer gave, but White has a surprising resource here. The queen can return home, pinning the bishop and threatening to capture the pawn at e5. 15.Qd1! e4 (15...Re8; 16.Bg5 Qe6; 17.Nfxe5+) 16.Bg5! Qe6; 17.Nfe5+ Ke8; 18.Nxd6+ cxd6; 19.Nxc6 where Black's pawns are simply too weak. Amusingly, White threatens to return the queen to a4, setting deadly threats.

**12...dxe5; 13.Nxe5!** The knight cannot be captured because the queen would be pinned after Re1. Black's queenside weaknesses are just part of the problem. The real suffering is caused by the lack of kingside development and his wide open king.

**13...Bd6.** 13...O-O-O; 14.Qe2 Kb7; 15.Nb3 is, as Fischer put it, "murderous" because of the threat of Na5+. **14.Nxg6 Qxg6.** Opening up the h-file would not have helped, as Geller realized in despair, after thinking for half an hour. 14...hxg6 would have been countered by 15.Ne4! with a nasty fork. 15...Qh4; 16.Nxd6+ cxd6; 17.Qxd6 wins. Black does not have time to complete the kingside attack. 17...Qxh3? gets checkmated after 18.Re1+.

15.Re1+. The final onslaught begins. **15...Kf8.** 15...Kd8 doesn't get the king to safety. 16.Nc4 threatens Bf4. At least 15...Ne7 preserves castling options, but 16.Nc4 O-O-O 17.Qa4 is going to clobber the queenside. **16.Nc4 h5.**

Black hopes for a kingside attack, but it isn't going to happen without the assistance of the bishop at d6, which is quickly removed from the board. **17.Nxd6 cxd6.** This undoubles the pawns, but it would have been better to take with the queen. 17...Qxd6; 18.Qxd6+ cxd6; 19.Bf4 Rd8 (19...d5? is refuted by 20.Bd6+) 20.Rad1 d5; 21.c4 hxg4; 22.hxg4 would have been just a bit better for White, but probably sufficient for Fischer to squeeze out a win.

**18.Bf4!** The pressure builds. The bishop also provides important defense for the kingside, since it can take up a position at g3 if necessary. 18...d5? Played after another long thoughtful pause that lasted forty minutes according to Fischer. **18...Rd8** was suggested right after the game by World Champion Tal, but analysis led to a cute win for White. 19.Qe2 hxg4; 20.hxg4 leaves Black with no useful move. The queen, knight and one rook have to stay in place to guard against immediate checkmates at e7 and e8. Perhaps Tal had a point, though. Suppose Black launches his own attack by putting pressure on the pawn at g4? 20...f5!?; 21.Rad1 and only now 21...d5!? White can probably win by moving the rook to d4, followed by moving it leftwards to a4, and finally capturing at a6. 22.Rd4 Qxg4+; 23.Qxg4 fxg4; 24.Ra4 looks like a very promising pawn sacrifice. **19.Qb3.**

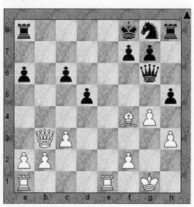

**19...hxg4.** Geller spent over half an hour on this move, too. He was contemplating the unpleasant consequences of defending the pawn at d6 with his knight, but in each case Fischer had a devastating reply available. Desperation was truly justified. 19... Ne7 loses to an elegant exchange sacrifice. 20.Rxe7 Kxe7; 21.Qb7+

Kf6; 22.Qxc6+ Ke7; 23.Re1+ with a forced mate in seven moves. 19...Nf6; 20.Qb7 Re8; 21.Rxe8+ Nxe8; 22.Re1 forces 22...Qf6 but 23.Qb8 wins easily. **20.Qb7.** Geller gets to toss a check, but he can't cash it and quickly gives up. **20...gxh3+; 21.Bg3 Rd8; 22.Qb4+** Black **resigned.**

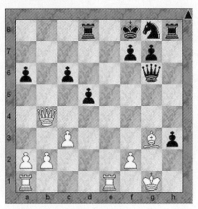

Black's king ends up trapped at f8.

**Game notes:** Although Bobby didn't win the event, his second place finish was still a stunning success for a teenager. In this game, Fischer plays an excellent move (Bf4) that simultaneously attacks and defends. His opponent, Mikhail Tal, was at the time the youngest World Champion in history, having taken the title in 1960. His reign was also the shortest, as he returned the title to Botvinnik after losing their 1961 rematch.

# IT'S TOUGH TO DEFEND

**THE PLAYERS**
Bobby Fischer (White)
vs.
Viktor Korchnoi (U.S.S.R.)

**THE LOCATION**
The Interzonal,
in Stockholm, Sweden,
on 2/27/1962

## LESSON: KEEP THE PRESSURE ON AND YOUR OPPONENT MAY CRACK

Every sport has a concept of "pressure," though it is never easy to define. In chess, pressure is applied by attacking enemy forces, even when the enemy position is well defended. The more possible captures you have, the easier it is for your opponent to make a mistake and leave something unguarded.

Another type of pressure is the "forced move." It would seem that having no choice actually relieves some pressure, but psychologically it is annoying to have to play a particular move with no plausible alternative. A check will at least limit the options, though a check should be used only if all of the replies lead to positions that are better for the attacker than before.

Keep the pressure on by placing your pieces where they attack multiple enemy targets. Aim your pieces at the king, so that your opponent will have to keep attacking forces back home on defense. The concept of pressure is often seen in the Spanish Inquisition, as some Closed Variations of the Spanish Game (Ruy Lopez) are often called. Black can handle the pressure with excellent play, but when Bobby Fischer was White, most couldn't stand it. The result was usually a costly error, which Bobby exploited to win the game.

**1.e4 e5; 2.Nf3 Nc6; 3.Bb5 a6; 4.Ba4 Nf6; 5.O-O Be7; 6.Re1 b5; 7.Bb3 O-O; 8.c3 d6; 9.d4.**

Once again Bobby finds himself on the White side of the Spanish Inquisition. Normally, White plays 9.h3 in this variation to prevent Black's bishop from getting to g4 and pinning the knight at f3. The plan of storming the center was worked out early in the 20th century by Frederick Yates, and revived many decades later by a gambit developed by Oleg Romanishin. Personally, I have always liked the line for White and have played it many times.

**9...Bg4; 10.Be3 exd4.** Fischer considered 10...d5 to be a better choice, but over forty years later it has a poor reputation and is not seen frequently. The capture at d4, Korchnoi's choice, remains the main line. **11.cxd4 Na5.** 11...d5!?; 12.e5 Ne4; 13.Nc3 (or 13.Nbd2 Na5) 13...Nxc3; 14.bxc3 Qd7 is considered about equal. Bobby thought that moving the knight to d2 instead of c3 was good enough for an advantage for White. This was the prevailing view at the time, so Korchnoi followed a more traditional path.

**12.Bc2 Nc4.** A tempting move, often played, but Black would have done better to play 12...c5. This was Fischer's preference, and it remains the theoretically approved move. **13.Bc1 c5; 14.b3 Na5.** 14...Nb6, popular back in 1962, falls a bit short of equality after 15.Nbd2 Rc8; 16.h3 Bh5; 17.d5, closing the center and leaving Black a bit cramped.

**15.d5!** It pays to study the classics! With this move, Fischer improved on the famous game Capablanca vs. Bogoljubow, from the 1922 International tournament in London. That game delayed the advance of the d-pawn for one more move, but that gave Black additional defensive options. 15.Bb2 was met in that game by the dynamic knight maneuver 15...Nc6! 16.d5 Nb4! By advancing the d-pawn right away, Fischer eliminates the possibility of a knight retreat to c6.

**15...Nd7.** 15...Nxe4; 16.Rxe4 Bxf3; 17.Qxf3 Bf6 doesn't win the rook at a1 because of 18.Nc3 and if 18...b4, then 19.Bb2 bxc3; 20.Bxc3 Bxc3; 21.Qxc3. Fischer rightly claimed a big advantage for White.

**16.Nbd2 Bf6; 17.Rb1.** This position has actually been reached many times, and usually 17...Bc3 or 17...Ne5 are played. Korchnoi later said that the latter move was to be preferred, though Fischer thought that it was already too late for Black to equalize in the line. Korchnoi was certainly correct in labeling his own move as "overambitious."

**17...c4?!; 18.h3 Bxf3.** If the bishop retreats, it is kicked again by g4, and then the White knight can find a path to g3 via f1, a typical Spanish maneuver, **19.Nxf3 cxb3; 20.axb3 Qc7; 21.Be3?!** Some analysts, including Korchnoi himself, considered this an error, preferring 21.Re2. Fischer didn't consider it a big deal. In his opinion, White's advantage is small in any case. The point is that after 21...Bc3; 22.Nd4 White is a tempo up. The same position is reached as in the game but with White on the move instead of Black.

**21...Bc3!; 22.Re2 b4.** Black has some play on the dark squares, but still has more weaknesses and an offside knight. Black is going to have to spend some time coordinating the forces, which suggested to Bobby that it might be a good time to launch an attack. **23.Nd4 Rfe8?!** 23...g6 was the correct move. White would have a hard time demonstrating any significant advantage after 24.Bd3 Nc5; 25.Ra2 Nab7; 26.Ne2 Bg7 despite some pressure on the queenside. **24.Nf5 Nb7; 25.Bd4!** White challenges the annoying enemy bishop, while also aiming at g7.

**25...g6.** The pawn is defended, but now there is a hole in the Black kingside. Still, exchanging bishops would have given White a tremendous knight at d4. **26.Nh6+ Kf8; 27.Rc1!**

Aiming the rook at the enemy queen is a clever tactic which can lead to great rewards if the opponent isn't careful. **27...Rac8; 28.Bd3 Qa5.** Wisely stepping out of the line of fire of the enemy rook. **29.Rec2 Ne5; 30.Bf1 Nc5!** Korchnoi has transferred his knights from passive positions into very active positions. It costs him a pawn, but he certainly has some compensation for it.

**31.Bxc3 bxc3; 32.Rxc3 Kg7; 33.Ng4 Nxg4; 34.Qxg4.** By exchanging pieces and getting rid of Black's knight at e5, Bobby has reduced the level of compensation and has a substantial advantage.

But the pressure at e4 does give him some counterplay. The knight at c5 is much stronger than the bishop.

**34...Rb8; 35.Rf3?!** Fischer's only comment is to quote Korchnoi: "White's best chance is to revive his attack on the King's wing." True enough! Bobby plans Qf4 on the next move. But it would have been better to switch the order of moves. If he had played 35.Qf4! first, then on 35...Nxe4 he would have had 36.Rc7!, attacking the pawn at f7 more effectively from the side.

**35...Nxe4; 36.Qf4 f5.** Although this move does weaken the king's barrier, it isn't a problem because White can't get a rook to c7. Alternatively, Black could just have advanced one of the rooks to the second rank. That would've been safer in the long run. Fischer admitted that the kingside weakness couldn't be exploited.

**37.Re3 Re5; 38.Rc6 Rbe8.** Korchnoi should be thinking about kicking White's queen with ...g5. In his habitual time pressure, Korchnoi simply overlooked Bobby's reply. The rules required getting past move forty before the player's allotted time expired. In those days, each player had a generous two and a half hours to complete the first forty moves. Now it is generally two hours.

38...g5!?; 39.Qf3 Rbe8; 40.Rxa6 Qxd5; 41.b4 would have left the players with roughly even chances, according to Fischer. White's passed pawn is easier to advance and his king is safer, but that only adds up to a small advantage.

**39.Rxd6!** Korchnoi didn't overlook the pin on the knight at d4, but did overlook a fork at the end of the combination, which is seen in the variation.

**39...Qa1?** Both players agree that this was the fatal mistake. The pin on the bishop at f1, combined with the defense of the rook at e5, seem to add up to the right plan.

Black also has to avoid 39...Nxd6?; 40.Rxe5 Rxe5; 41.Qxe5+ Kh6; 42.Qxd6 with an extra bishop for White.

However, there was a more active, and fairly obvious alternative. Black can drive back the enemy queen. 39...g5!; 40.Rd7+ Kg6; 41.Qf3 Qb6 is Fischer's line. The rook at d7 can be trapped easily since it has no support and no escape route. Fischer solved the problem tactically, by threatening the pawn at a6. 42.Qe2!

42...Nxf2! Black has resources too. The advantage of lining up the queen against the enemy king is seen. It sets the stage for pins. For example, if White were to capture the knight with the king, then Black would advance the f-pawn to f4 and exploit the pin to win the rook. 43.Rxe5 is forced. 43...Ne4+; 44.Kh2 Rxe5; 45.Qxa6 Qxa6; 46.Bxa6 Nf6. The final fork wins back the d-pawn, and leads to an endgame which should result in a draw, though White has many winning chances.

**40.Rxa6.** Korchnoi just has to make one more move to reach the time control, but the game is now utterly lost.

**40...Qd4; 41.Rd3 Qb2; 42.d6 g5; 43.Qe3 f4; 44.Qa7+.** Korchnoi **resigned.**

# AIMING FOR THE FRIED LIVER

**THE PLAYERS**

Bobby Fischer (White)
vs.
Arthur Bisguier (U.S.A.)

**THE LOCATION**

The New York State Open Championship, in New York, U.S.A., on 9/1/1963

## LESSON: TACTICS: THE BUILDING BLOCKS OF VICTORY

Tactics are the means by which we gain strategic goals. Tactics are the little maneuvers that can significantly improve the position. They can be bundled into "combinations" that result in a decisive material gain or even checkmate.

To say tactics are important is one thing. Sure, you can improve your tactical skills by doing exercises and studying guides (see my book Killer Chess Tactics). But even after you have learned all of the basic tactical tricks, how do you use them in a game?

This is one of the most frustrating areas for beginners. Sometimes they notice immediately after making a move that the opponent can use a pin, fork or other trick to win a piece, or worse.

My advice to beginners is to always look for all captures and checks on every move. It doesn't mean that these moves should be played! By simply looking at all possible captures and checks, you can get a sense of what tactics might be available. You are placing these ingredients into your mental cooking pot so that a nice tactical meal can be served up later. When it is your opponent's move, look for all possible enemy captures and checks, too.

**1.e4 e5; 2.Nf3 Nc6; 3.Bc4.** Fischer chooses the Italian Game, instead of his favorite Spanish Game (3.Bb5). Most professional players prefer the more subtle Spanish approach, rather than aiming at Black's weak f7-square immediately. **3...Nf6; 4.Ng5.**

This traditional line of the Italian Game has always been considered amateurish. It is seen mostly in scholastic games and games by beginners. There isn't any particular reason for this prejudice. Once in a while a superstar will use the line, usually quite effectively.

**4...d5.** The approved reaction. Black sacrifices a pawn to eliminate the pressure, hoping either to regain it later or obtain some kind of compensation. The only alternatives, 4...Bc5 and 4...Nxe5, are both considered dubious, although each has some passionate fans at amateur levels. **5.exd5 Na5.**

The main line, known as the Polerio Variation, has been around for hundreds of years. Black doesn't recapture the pawn at d5, because that would lead to a vicious sacrifice at f7, known as the "Fried Liver Attack." Indeed, that attack has been known to destroy Black's position on scholastic chess boards all over the world. Beginners soon learn to put it aside, in favor of this move, or 5...Nd4 or 5...b5 which lead to very exciting complications but are generally considered less reliable.

**6.Bb5+ c6; 7.dxc6 bxc6.** This is the traditional line, though John Watson and I, in our book Survive and Beat Annoying Chess

Openings, also recommend 7…Bd7 to players of the Black side. Substantial analysis of the line seen in this game is also presented in that book. **8.Be2.** This position is often seen in games between players who are beyond the beginner stage at chess. It is how Black is supposed to handle the defense, according to an overwhelming majority of theoreticians. Black is down a pawn, but can develop quickly. Black also has greater control of the center. Still, White has an extra pawn.

**8…h6.** Black sensibly kicks out the invading knight. After it retreats, what has become of White's impressive attacking formation seen in the first few moves? That's why the Ng5 attack hold less appeal to more experienced players. The rapid attacks against the uncastled Black king rarely materialize once players have learned to avoid the traps.

**9.Nh3!?** In Fischer's 60 Memorable Games, Larry Evans writes that this move was "found wanting at the turn of the century, and perhaps best left there. Fischer was influenced by Steinitz, and borrows the idea. In my view, 9.Nh3 is at least as good as any of the alternatives, though White can't hope for any substantial advantage out of the opening."

**9…Bc5.** Black usually plays this or Steinitz's 9…Bd6, which might be best. Bisguier must have been caught by surprise; the move 9.Nh3 had not been seen in serious chess in over 70 years! In the same year, Fischer's friend Bernie Zuckerman played in a World Student team competition. Capturing the knight disrupts White's kingside, but it isn't worth giving up the bishop for that knight.

**10.O-O.** Fischer follows Steinitz, but remarked later that 9.d3 is superior, and he backed it up by playing the move a few rounds later vs. Radoicic, a game he also won. **10...O-O; 11.d3.** White must settle for this unambitious move, because Black owns the d4-square.

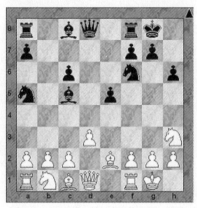

**11...Bxh3.** 11...Nb7 is now considered best, though it is unmentioned by Fischer, who said that while Bisguier's move was an improvement over one of the Steinitz vs. Chigorin games, 11...Nh7, credited to Gottschall, deserved consideration.

**12.gxh3 Qd7.** Black's development is almost complete. Bisguier has a pawn in the center. His rooks can "see" each other. The knight at a5 is still offside, but it has a path to the kingside via b7-d6-f5. White has not developed the queenside, and his pawn at h3 is a weakling that can be swept off the board by the enemy queen. Yet the position is considered by most authorities to be slightly in White's favor! As you'll see, Black's pieces need a lot of time to create serious threats. White can bring the pieces from the queenside to the kingside without difficulty. And the half-open g-file can be a pathway for an attack. **13.Bf3 Qxh3; 14.Nd2 Rad8; 15.Bg2!**

The bishop is brought to a great position, defending the king while keeping pressure at c6. The knight can get to f3, and Fischer can bring the bishop to e3 to counter the influence of the enemy bishop at c5.

**15...Qf5.** The queen should perhaps have retreated to e6, defending c6, so that the knight could find a way back into the game. 15...Qh4? would have been a serious mistake. 16.Nf3 Qh5; 17.Qe1 is a double attack against the pawn at e5 and the knight at a5, thanks to the presence of the knight at f3. **16.Qe1.** Fischer later thought that Qf3, heading for a superior endgame, might have been a better choice. **16...Rfe8; 17.Ne4 Bb6; 18.Nxf6+.** 18.b4 Nb7; 19.b5 would have been sharper, according to Fischer. The point is the threat of Nxf6+ followed by Bxb7, if Black captures at b5. 19...Nd5; 20.bxc6 Na5 is suggested by Huebner, who says that Black has nothing to worry about. Indeed, I'd prefer to be playing Black in this position. **18...Qxf6; 19.Kh1.**

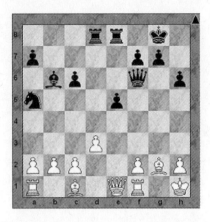

**19...c5.** Bisguier sensibly tries to get this knight back into the game. It is true that the knight is needed for defense, but there are some immediate problems that need attention. Fischer wants to blast open the f-file with f4. Black could have prevented this.

19...g5! was the right move. Black would then have achieved full equality. 20.Qc3 c5; 21.Be3 could have been met by 21...Nc6!; 22.Bxc5 Nd4 threatening a fork at e2. After 23.Bxd4 Bxd4 the queen must go to a3, as otherwise the b-pawn is lost either immediately or after ...Rb8. 24.Qa3 e4 creates a double attack against b2, and Black can safely capture the f-pawn if White plays c3.

**20.Qc3!?** A triple attack against the enemy knight, c-pawn and e-pawn. It also sets up a threat, as will be seen on the next move. The move has been highly praised, and Bobby himself marked it with "!," indicating that it is a good move.

Huebner presents detailed analysis showing that Black is not at a disadvantage in this position, and could have kept the balance by pushing the c-pawn as a temporary sacrifice. 20.Bd2 has been the subject of a great deal of attention. Huebner evaluates the position even after 20...Nc6; 21.Qe4 Nd4; 22.c3 Nf5; 23.Rad1. Perhaps Fischer's move was not absolutely best, in an objective sense.

Part of Fischer's success was due to his uncanny ability to set problems for his opponents that they were not able to solve. Sitting at home with a powerful computer assistant, it is possible to find errors even in the analysis of one of the greatest players of all time. A small degree of subjectivity is often seen in the writings of the greatest players. Their confidence at the board comes from an internal confidence. Sometimes that surfaces in writings or public comments. I don't think it in any way diminishes the value of their comments.

**20...Nc6?** The obvious move, getting the knight back into the game. Fischer points out that g5 would come too late, but there was another move which could have been tried, with more chances for success. 20...g5 doesn't stop 21.f4! because 21...gxf4 22.Bxf4 exploits the pin against the pawn at e5. If the pawn takes the bishop, then White simply captures the Black queen at f6. 20...c4!; 21.dxc4 Rc8 regains the pawn, and Black has better development and a strong initiative.

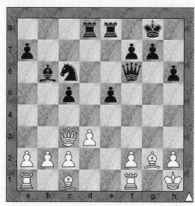

**21.f4! Nd4; 22.Qc4.** Black's position is ugly, with a "tall pawn" sitting at b6. Still, the knight occupies a powerful position and White doesn't have any obvious targets. **22...Qg6; 23.c3 Nf5.**

23...Nc2 isn't mentioned, but Black might be able to maneuver the queen to e2, for example 24.f5 Qh5; 25.Rb1 Qe2 with the threat of ...Ne3. So White probably has to head for the endgame. 26.Qe4 Qxe4; 27.Bxe4. Then Black has to sacrifice the c-pawn to get the knight out. 27...c4; 28.dxc4 Ne3; 29.Bxe3 Bxe3; 30.Rbd1 Rxd1; 31.Rxd1 with an extra pawn for White. The queenside pawn mass should prove decisive, though the bishops of opposite color will give Black chances for a draw.

23...Ne2; 24.f5 Qf6; 25.Be4 is "tremendous," according to Fischer. I'm not at all convinced. 25...Qh4 sets up the threat of ...Ng3+, forking king, rook and bishop. White's bishop at e4 is pinned to the queen. Looks about even to me.

**24.fxe5 Rxe5; 25.Bf4 Re2.** 25...Ne3; 26.Bxe3 Rxe3 would have been even, but Bisguier aims to take a full point from his young opponent. His position allows such optimistic play, provided that he doesn't get too greedy. **26.Be4.**

**26...Rxb2?** This is simply a blunder, which costs Bisguier the game. He failed to recognize the precarious position of the knight at f5, which is pinned to the queen. 26...Re8; 27.Bf3 Rxb2 was the accurate plan. White has some compensation for the pawn in the bishop pair, especially since the bishop at g6 is useless.

**27.Be5!** Bisguier reacted visibly to this move, which he had clearly overlooked. Resignation would be appropriate here, but Bisguier let the public see the point before giving up. **27...Re8; 28.Rxf5 Rxe5; 29.Rxe5.** Black **resigned.** The queen is attacked and if it runs away, then White has a back rank checkmate at e8.

# GAME #12

# THE CASE OF THE WRONG ROOK

**THE PLAYER**
Robert Byrne (U.S.A.)
vs.
Bobby Fischer (Black)

**THE LOCATION**
United States Championship,
in New York, U.S.A.,
on 12/18/1963

## LESSON: CHOOSE YOUR ROOK PLACEMENT CAREFULLY!

If you play the opening properly, once your rooks are connected you will start thinking about moving one or both of them to the center of the Board. The problem is that there are often three or four squares (d1, e1, and c1, or f1) that all might be profitably used by the rook. Students often tell me that the decision of where to place the rooks is one of the most difficult they encounter.

But it's not just a problem for students. In fact, even the world's best players often falter when faced with the critical decision of where to place the rooks. There aren't any magic formulas or incantations that can guide you to the correct solution. But even a beginner can improve replacement by thinking seriously about the future of each rook.

For example, if you intend to push a pawn forward, a rook might be very useful behind that pawn. You'll see many games in this collection where rooks are best used on open files. In other games you'll see that rooks can line up against any teams and queens even if there are a lot of pieces in the way. Your plan then will be to get the pieces out of the way so the rooks can do their thing.

Prophecy is tricky business, as our game will show. After castling, Byrne delays a decision on the rooks, and both find themselves in awkward positions. An incorrect choice gets him into serious trouble.

**1.d4 Nf6; 2.c4 g6; 3.g3 c6; 4.Bg2 d5.** Black has transposed to the Gruenfeld Defense. Because of White's formation, we have what is known as a Neo-Gruenfeld. Black has finally placed a pawn in the center, so White will not be able to dominate that region of the board as in the King's Indian, where Black plays the more modest ...d6 instead of ...d5. **5.cxd5 cxd5; 6.Nc3 Bg7.**

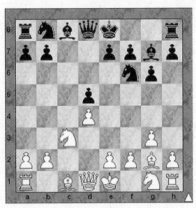

**7.e3.** This is not a particularly ambitious move. Fischer was on the Black side against Benko, and faced the normal, and more promising move 7.Nf3. That game ended in a quick draw. **7...O-O; 8.Nge2 Nc6; 9.O-O b6.**

The bishop is headed for a6, where it will dominate a long diagonal, and pin the knight at e2 to the rook at f1. **10.b3.** Having played e3, White also has to develop the bishop on the queenside. **10...Ba6; 11.Ba3 Re8.** Black has also played the logical 11...Qd7, which connects the rooks. Both are useful moves that have served Black well in this position. **12.Qd2.**

**12...e5!** 12...e6 is passive. White can take advantage of this by preparing action on the c-file. Complete symmetry usually runs into trouble if carried too far. In this case, White plays 13.Rfc1! This is the right rook. White unpins the knight at e2, which can get to f4 and set up some nice tricks. 13...Rc8; 14.Nf4 was agreed drawn in one game, but another saw White gain the upper hand after 14...Bf8; 15.Bxf8 Rxf8; 16.h4 Qe7; 17.Qb2 Rc7 where in Dizdar vs. Cepon, at Ljubljana 1995 the Grandmaster playing White could have gone in for 18.Bxd5! since 18...exd5; 19.Ncxd5 Nxd5; 20.Nxd5 Qd8; 21.Nxc7 Qxc7; 22.Qc3 Bb7; 23.d5 exploits the pin and wins a piece.

**13.dxe5.** 13.Rac1 exd4; 14.exd4 Rc8 was possible, and Fischer looked at 15.f3, though Huebner counters with 15...b5! He suggests 15.Rfe1 instead. **13...Nxe5; 14.Rfd1?**

This is a classic example of moving the wrong rook to the right square. It was only natural to want to get out from under the pin. The knight at e2 will now be able to move. The problem is that Byrne failed to consider the importance of the potential pin of the knight at c3 by the bishop at g7, which is hidden by the knights at e5 and f6. In the future, these knights can quickly get out of the way. Byrne felt the pressure of the pin on the a6-f1 diagonal but not on the a1-h8 diagonal. The effect won't be seen for another five moves, but it is fatal.

14.Rad1 is better, eliminating the danger on the long diagonal. There was a great deal of debate about the proper continuation after this move. 14...Qd7; 15.Bb2 Qg4; 16.f3 Qd7 might give Black a "minuscule" advantage, according to Huebner. Fischer, as usual, claimed much more for Black, but that is really just a sign of his optimistic nature.

**14...Nd3.**

**15.Qc2.** Bobby felt that White's position is pretty much toast here, but Huebner found an alternative that isn't too awful for White. 15.Nd4 Ne4; 16.Nxe4 dxe4 17.Bb2 Rc8; 18.a4 where White at least has some counterplay on the queenside.

**15...Nxf2!** A classic sacrifice against the most vulnerable defender of the White king. **16.Kxf2 Ng4+; 17.Kg1 Nxe3.**

Bobby already has two pawns for the knight, and now by forking three White pieces, Black can at least pick up the exchange. **18.Qd2 Nxg2!** The bishop is a more important defender of the king than the rook at d1, so Fischer removes it. **19.Kxg2 d4!**

The pawn advances, and if White moves the knight at c3, then the knight at e2 will fall to the rook with check, supported by the bishop. The advance has another venomous point. The long diagonal a8-h1 is now open for business.

**20.Nxd4 Bb7+!; 21.Kf1.** The inferior 21.Kg1 Bxd4+; 22.Qxd4 allows a neat trick. 22...Re1+! is strong, because the rook is taboo. If it is captured, the queen at d4 has no support. 23.Kf2 Qxd4+; 24.Rxd4 Rxa1 gives Black a decisive material advantage.

**21...Qd7.** The invasion of the light squares is in full swing, and there is no way White can survive. So Byrne **resigned.**

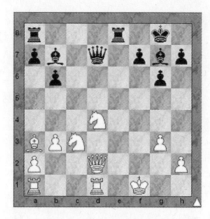

Bobby wasn't too happy with the capitulation, because he wanted to finish the game brilliantly with 22.Qf2 Qh3+; 23.Kg1 Re1+!! This deflects the rook from the defense of d4. White can't capture with the queen because of mate at g2. 24.Rxe1 Bxd4; 25.Qxd4 Qg2. Checkmate.

**Game notes:** This game won the Best Game Prize for the event, deservedly so. Not that Fischer needed any more kudos after his incredible perfect tournament. He won all eleven games, and his opponents were by no means pushovers. It was the United States Championship after all! Robert Byrne is the brother of Donald Byrne, Fischer's opponent in our first game.

# WHEN PREPARATIONS BACKFIRE

## THE PLAYERS
Bobby Fischer (White)
vs.
Robert Steinmeyer (U.S.A.)

## THE LOCATION
The United States Championship,
in New York, U.S.A.,
on 12/22/1963

## LESSON: DON'T TRUST OPENING THEORY!

This advice seems strange coming from a writer of dozens of books on opening theory, but it is true. Chess "theory" refers to the collective wisdom of the chess community as reflected in writing and games. In the time before reliable computer analysis, opening theory had to be rewritten frequently as proposals and evaluations underwent practical tests.

Computer analysis has eliminated many of the purely tactical errors found in virtually all opening books written before the 21st century. Unfortunately, reliance on computers has also led to less research of old books. So many times, good advice in ancient texts has been overlooked. Sometimes these suggestions and calculations that even computers still can't handle them.

Increasingly, professional games are decided by moves developed in a home laboratory. Finding holes in published analysis is part of the professional arsenal these days. Sometimes the preparation boomerangs, as in my example.

Beginners and intermediate players should always keep in mind the basic opening principles in the first lesson. Most of your opponents won't be playing long prepared variations. The moves you learn in books may be rare in your own games at that level.

**1.e4 c6; 2.d4 d5; 3.Nc3 dxe4; 4.Nxe4 Bf5.** The classical Caro-Kann is a solid and respected defense, favored by many strong players. Several World Champions used it regularly, including Smyslov, Tal, and especially Karpov.

**5.Ng3 Bg6; 6.Nf3 Nf6.** It is uncommon to play this so early. **7.h4 h6; 8.Bd3.** 8.Ne5! is a more effective move as Spassky showed in his match against Petrosian in1966. **8...Bxd3; 9.Qxd3 e6; 10.Bd2 Nbd7.** Play has returned to the normal main line of the Classical Caro-Kann.

10...Qc7!?; 11.c4 Nbd7; 12.Bc3 would have transposed to Fischer vs. Donner, Varna Olympiad 1962, a game that Black was no doubt familiar with, but Fischer seemed to get a very good position there and Steinmeyer had a specific variation in mind.

**11.O-O-O.**

Black now has to decide which flank will be home to his king. For a long time Black almost automatically castled queenside after ... Qc7, as in this game. Toward the end of the millennium, plans with ...Be7 and kingside castling became much more common. The difference is one of style. Opposite wing castling leads to more attacking play than castling on the same side. **11...Qc7; 12.c4 O-O-O.** 12...Bd6 was preferred by Fischer, who analyzed 13.Ne4 Bf4! The removal of the dark square bishops would solve Black's opening problems.

**13.Bc3!** Naturally, Bobby sidesteps the liberating exchange. Now Steinmeyer reveals his plan, but it turns out that it is nothing to be afraid of. **13...Qf4+?** Checks are often best kept in reserve. Once cashed, they are gone. The queen should have stayed at c7 for defense. 13...Bd6!; 14.Ne4 Bf4+; 15.Kb1 Ne5! exploits the pin on the d-file to gain equality. **14.Kb1 Nc5?** The queen should simply have returned home. But although this is a bad move, you can't blame Steinmeyer. He was following a prepared line in which he had good reason to be confident. **15.Qc2.**

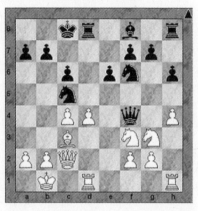

**15...Nce4.** This position had already been reached in Shamkovich vs. Goldberg, USSR 1961, where White continued ineffectively. **16.Ne5!** 16.Ba5? was played in the Shamkovich game. Steinmeyer no doubt was quite pleased with the prospect of meeting that variation. But Fischer's improvement destroys the entire variation with the check at f4. I had a similar experience in a very important game, and can appreciate exactly how Steinmeyer must have felt. To come so close to unleashing a powerful new move, just to have the whole variation blown out of the water, is very painful.

**16...Nxf2.** The knight had various captures available.

16...Nxg3; 17.fxg3 Qxg3 would have lost to 18.Rd3 Qf4; 19.Rf3 Qe4; 20.Nxf7 as pointed out by Fischer.

16...Nxc3+ is handled by 17.bxc3! The queen capture would leave the f-pawn unguarded. 17...Rg8 might have been the reply, so if the White knight grabs the f-pawn, at least there isn't a fork of both rooks. 18.Rd3 h5; 19.Rf3 is what Bobby had in mind, ready to meet 19...Qh6 with 20.Nxf7 forking the rook and queen.

Psychologically, Steinmeyer must already have been devastated. Reacting to an unexpected opening novelty is always difficult. The game, previously dictated by Black, is suddenly being run by White. Was this a prepared move by Fischer? There's no way for Black to know.

**17.Rdf1!** A killer pin forced Black to give up.

Black **resigned**, because of 17...Qxg3; 18.Rxf2 Qe3; 19.Re2 Qf4; 20.Nxf7 with a killer fork.

**Game notes:** Though Fischer's opponent was "thoroughly" prepared, his planned trap backfires, leading to an easy victory en route to his 11-0 finish.

# CHOKING ON A PAWN

## THE PLAYERS
Bobby Fischer (White)
vs.
Pal Benko (U.S.A.)

## THE LOCATION
The United States Championship,
in New York U.S.A.,
on 12/30/1963

## LESSON: LOCKING DOWN THE ENEMY FORCES

Even when your opponent has forces in position to defend the king, you can often attack successfully if you can limit their usefulness. We use the term "mobility" to describe the number of squares a piece can reach in one move.

Defensive pieces need to be mobile because they can often come under attack. One useful formation combines kingside castling with a fianchetto formation. The g-pawn advances to g6, and the bishop occupies the hole at g7. The knight usually goes to f6. When the knight is mobile, it can quickly get out of the way so that the bishop can take aim on the long diagonal.

If the position is weakened, however, the mobility drops quickly. Remove the pawn at g6, and the bishop will have to stay at g7 to guard the king against attack on the g-file. Or the king will have to move to h8 or f8, taking away a square from the bishop. The knight cannot maintain its position at f6, because it can be attacked along the f-file and also by a bishop at g5 or knight at d5.

In our game, Fischer accomplishes the strategic goal of eliminating the defending pawn, and suddenly Black's pieces find themselves in awkward positions.

**1.e4 g6; 2.d4 Bg7.**

Benko chooses the "Modern Defense," which can later move into territory of well-known openings such as the King's Indian Defense or Pirc Defense.

**3.Nc3.** Fischer chooses to keep the game in the king pawn group by resisting the temptation to play 3.c4, which would create a big center but allow Black to switch to Fischer's own favorite, the King's Indian Defense, by playing …Nf6. **3…d6; 4.f4.** This is known as the Austrian Attack. The f-pawn can be used as a battering ram at f5, leading to open lines for White's dark-square bishop and possibly a rook at f1, especially if White castles on the kingside. **4… Nf6; 5.Nf3 O-O; 6.Bd3.**

**6...Bg4?** This is considered an error. Although the pin on the knight is strong, White can force matters on the kingside. Instead, Black usually develops the knight from b8 to c6 or a6. From a6, it can support the advance of the c-pawn to c5. This can also be played immediately. 6...c5; 7.dxc5 dxc5; 8.e5 Nd5; 9.Nxd5 Qxd5; 10.Qe2 gives White a bit more space, but Black has no problems developing and it isn't easy for White to make progress.

**7.h3! Bxf3; 8.Qxf3 Nc6; 9.Be3 e5.**

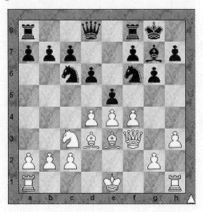

Black's strategy is to strike at White's big center, hoping the pawns will turn out to be weak. This move was necessary, as otherwise White might advance to e5 first.

**10.dxe5.** Fischer opens up the d-file for future use, and eliminates the threat faced by the pawn when it was still at d4, attacked by both knight and pawn. **10...dxe5; 11.f5!** Fischer advances into enemy territory by sending a single soldier, but the g-pawn may soon join its comrade. Black's problem is a lack of targets. There is simply no counter-play, and it is clear that the Black strategy has failed to materialize.

**11...gxf5?** This capture was soon abandoned and replaced by a more active plan, bringing the knight to d4, where it attacks the queen. **12.Qxf5 Nd4; 13.Qf2!**

Fischer could have grabbed the pawn at e5. 13.Qxe5 Ng4 is a double attack on the White queen. 14.Qxg7+ Kxg7; 15.hxg4 was tempting, but Fischer felt that after 15...Nc6 it would be difficult to make progress. For example, on 16.Bh6+ Kh8; 17.Bxf8 Qxf8; 18.O-O-O, White has a rook, bishop and pawn for the queen, but White has three weak pawns and the bishop isn't of much use. After 18...Ne5 Black has a strong blockade, and a clear advantage.

**13...Ne8.** An odd station for the knight, but it does defend g7, and can come to d6 or return to f6 as needed. Otherwise White simply castles on the queenside, moves the knight, and drives out the invader with c3. On the other hand, the kingside is a bit congested and Black's forces aren't very mobile.

**14.O-O.** Fischer chooses king safety over a kingside pawnstorm. Sensing a touch of conservative play by the aggressive Fischer, Benko decides to add tension to the position. Fischer was under a little pressure. Though he would clearly win the event, he was aiming for his perfect score!

**14...Nd6!?.** 14...c6; 15.Ne2 Nxe2+ is what Fischer was expecting. Then White's bishop pair and control of open lines would have given him an indisputable advantage. **15.Qg3 Kh8.** The king steps into the corner to avoid problems on the g-file, where White is ready to play Bh6. If Benko had chosen 15...f5, Bobby would have played 16.Bh6 Qf6; 17.Qxg7+ Qxg7; 18.Bxg7 Kxg7; 19.exf5

N6xf5; 20.Rae1 with a difficult endgame for Black. That e-pawn is a permanent weakness. Benko, an endgame specialist, wasn't about to suffer such torture, so decided to switch to defense.

**16.Qg4 c6?!** 16…c5 would have been wiser, intending to push the pawn and force White onto the defensive. **17.Qh5 Qe8?** 17…c5 was the best move, threatening to push back the bishop with …c4. Of course, this does give White access to d5 to capture the knight, but there was nothing better. **18.Bxd4 exd4.**

This position contains one of Fischer's most awesome moves. It seems that Black has things under control, because if White pushes the e-pawn there is a surprising defense. 19.e5? f5!; 20.Qxe8 Raxe8; 21.exd6 dxc3 is nothing special for White. Black's defense has too much mobility. When the f-pawn advances, the queen at e8 comes to life and is suddenly a valuable defender, confronting the White queen. If the f-pawn can be prevented from moving, then the mobility drops to near zero.

**19.Rf6!!** This move has been rightly praised as the ultimate blocking tactic. The rook is sacrificed just so that Black's f-pawn cannot advance, offering an exchange of queens that would put an end to White's attack. The tactic is knows as a "block."

**19…Kg8.** Otherwise checkmate is quickly achieved. For example: 19…Bxf6; 20.e5 Ne4; 21.Bxe4 h6; 22.Qxh6+ Kg8; 23.Qh7. Checkmate.

**20.e5 h6.** A final, desperate hope for a miracle. If White takes the knight with the rook, then the Black queen captures the pawn at e5, and, since the knight at c3 is still attacked by the pawn, Black would escape any serious damage. **21.Ne2!**

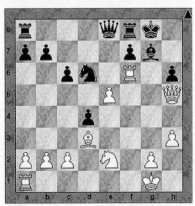

Benko **resigned**, because there is no way to effectively save the knight. Fischer threatened to move the queen to f5 and give mate at h7 if the knight abandons its post.

**Game notes:** Fischer didn't have to win this game to secure the United States Championship title, but he was aiming for the perfect 11-0 sweep. He played with full determination and created an absolute masterpiece, with one of his most memorable moves.

# ADVENTURES ALONG THE A-FILE

**THE PLAYERS**
Bobby Fischer (White)
vs.
Vassily Smyslov (U.S.S.R)

**THE LOCATION**
The Capablanca Memorial,
in Havana, Cuba,
on 6/26/1965

## LESSON: WEAK PAWNS ARE EXPLOITED BY OPENING LINES

When your opponent has weak pawns, you should try to aim rooks and bishops at them, operating from a distance. Later, knights can help out, but knights have to come to close to the pawns to be effective attackers. Often they can be kicked out before doing any damage.

If your long-range forces are aimed at the weak pawns, then a knight can deliver a decisive blow. You don't need knights, however. The pressure created by bishops and rooks creates problems for the opponent, no matter how well-defended the weak pawns seem to be.

Weak pawns in the center are vulnerable, because they can be attacked from all sides. Do not go after weak pawns right away. They are harder to defend in an endgame, when there are less pieces. Be patient; weak pawns are often fatal in endgames with just kings and pawns.

The endgame usually sees the king performing defensive duties for pawns, and the haughty king is a poor defender. In our game, Fischer shows just how painful pawn weaknesses can be. He superbly exploits these weaknesses by attacking with bishop, rook and knight.

**1.e4 e5; 2.Nf3 Nc6; 3.Bb5 a6; 4.Ba4 Nf6; 5.d3.** Fischer was a fan of some of Steinitz's opening ideas. Here he borrows another plan from First World Champion. The opening strategy is not very ambitious, but Bobby probably wanted to sidestep special opening analysis prepared by the Soviet "team."

**5...d6; 6.c3 Be7; 7.Nbd2 O-O.**

Smyslov is following traditional principles of development and has a very solid position. Fischer has chosen to delay castling, and takes advantage of the vacancy at f1 to reposition his knight at f1, heading to g3. This maneuver is usually seen only after White has castled and shifted the rook to e1.

**8.Nf1 b5; 9.Bb3 d5.** Bobby criticized this move as a waste of time, but it is considered just as good as the alternative strategy with ...Na5 and ...c5. White has spent enough time shuffling the knight that the maneuver d7-d6-d5 doesn't hurt. Indeed, Black is just two moves away from connecting the rooks and completing development while White has at least four steps to go. In addition, Black often plays the pawn first to d6, then to d5, in many variations. So Smyslov's choice is correct, despite Bobby's misgivings.

**10.Qe2 dxe4.** Fischer claimed that this move opens the position prematurely, but decades later, it remains the main line. Indeed, Black has more pieces in play and therefore benefits from a more open game. Bobby may have thought that such play by Black is a bit impudent, but his choice of a slow opening plan opened the door.

**11.dxe4 Be6!?** A bold choice by Smyslov, who offers Fischer the chance to double Black's pawns. However, Smyslov had good intuitions about such things, and the decision is correct. **12.Bxe6 fxe6; 13.Ng3 Qd7; 14.O-O.** 14.a4 leads to a messier position and during the game Fischer regretted that he didn't stroll down that path.

**14...Rad8.** Black owns the d-file, and will use it to swap queens. The resulting endgame is not in White's favor, despite Black's doubled pawns. However, the doubled pawns are weak. That is not a problem, as long as there are no other weak pawns to worry about, and lines remain closed. **15.a4 Qd3!; 16.Qxd3 Rxd3; 17.axb5 axb5; 18.Ra6!** This has to be played right away, as otherwise Black can play ...Bc5 and retreat to b6, eliminating the pressure on the 6th rank.

**18...Rd6.** This sets up a nice trick. Black can play ...Nd4, leading to a series of exchanges that eliminate any difficulties. **19.Kh1!**

Fischer anticipates Smyslov's plan and shifts his king to the corner, out of the checking range of a knight at d4. It is often useful to take time out to reposition the king so that the opponent can't throw a check.

Black now has four weak pawns: b5, c7, e5, e6. They aren't easy to get at, because there are no open files for attacking rooks, and White's bishop can't target them. The open a-file allows an attack from the side, but for the moment the knight at c6 prevents White from using the a5-square. Strategically, White needs to find a way to open lines and take aim at the weak pawns. Fischer eventually gets the idea, though it took him some time.

**19...Nd7?!** Here, and on the next move, Smyslov had a chance to take the initiative on the queenside by advancing the pawn to b4. Black's pawn at b5 is weak, but it is not under attack. Still, it is usually a good idea to get rid of weaknesses. Fischer doesn't manage to exploit this one for a long time, but in the end it is a significant cause of Black's demise.

**20.Be3 Rd8?!; 21.h3?!** Fischer wrote that at the time he just didn't appreciate the importance of the queenside situation. He could have easily restrained his target by playing b4, but doesn't get around to it until move 26.

**21...h6?!** Yet another opportunity for ...b4 slips by, and there won't be many more. **22.Rfa1.** By doubling rooks on the a-file,

Bobby prepares to invade Black's home ranks. **22...Ndb8.** Smyslov unleashes his own rook battery with the same goal. **23.Ra8 Rd1+; 24.Kh2 Rxa1; 25.Rxa1.**

**25...Nd7?** This was Smyslov's last chance to push the pawn. When he spoke to Fischer after the game by telephone, he already knew that it was his strategic mistake that cost him the game.

**26.b4!** Finally Bobby catches on, and insures that the weak pawn will remain in place. **26...Kf7.** Black supports his weak pawn at e6 with the king. This is appropriate in the endgame, where the absence of queens makes it hard for White to mount any serious attack on the king.

**27.Nf1.** The Spanish knight rarely backtracks to the queenside via its pivot square at f1! However, the action lies on the queenside, so the knight must get over there. **27...Bd6; 28.g3.**

Fischer liked to play with the initiative, but he always appreciated the importance of taking time to understand enemy threats and put an end to them. Black's arsenal included the possibility of ...Nd4, since if White captures it with the c-pawn, Black can recapture with the e-pawn, delivering a discovered check to the enemy king and picking off the bishop at e3. So Bobby planted the pawn at g3 to eliminate such tricks. **28...Nf6; 29.N1d2 Ke7; 30.Ra6.**

This forces Smyslov to set up a very passive, defensive position. He was already getting a bit depressed about his chances in the game. Though the position doesn't look all that bad, White's initiative is deadly.

**30...Nb8; 31.Ra5!** Now that the defender of a5 has retreated, the rook targets the unprotected pawn. 31...c6. Another small weakness is created. The sum of Black's little weaknesses is a big problem. **32.Kg2 Nbd7; 33.Kf1.** In the endgame, the king usually belongs in the center so that it can operate on either flank.

**33...Rc8?** A more active plan was available and this is just too passive. 33...Ne8! was the right move. The idea is to bring the knight to c7, then offer an exchange of rooks with ...Ra8. White still has a nagging advantage, but the game is not beyond salvation.

**34.Ne1!** Bobby spots the knight retreat first, and quickly prepares to get his knight to d3, after which the c-break will be effective. Black no longer has time to carry out the defensive maneuver mentioned in the previous note, though he does try. **34...Ne8; 35.Nd3 Nc7; 36.c4!**

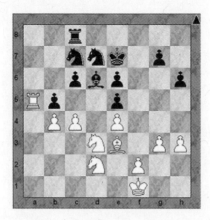

This perfectly timed break leads to a winning position. Black is just too tied down. Fischer keeps opening more lines while he establishes a powerful passed pawn on the queenside.

**36...bxc4; 37.Nxc4 Nb5; 38.Ra6.** Black's weak pawns are under tremendous pressure. **38...Kf6.** The Black king is tethered to the e-pawn, which needs defense. There was no alternative. 38...Nb8; 39.Ra8 Nc7 gets demolished by 40.Nxd6! Kxd6; 41.Bc5+ Kd7; 42.Nxe5+ and if 42...Kd8 there is the neat tactical trick 43.Rxb8! Rxb8; 44.Nxc6+ Kc8; 45.Nxb8 Kxb8; 46.Bd6 when the exchange of minor pieces leads to an easy winning king and pawn endgame.

**39.Bc1!** The bishop is repositioned so that it can strike at the weak pawn at e5. **39...Bb8; 40.Bb2.** Weak pawns on open lines are always good targets. That's the story of this game. **40...c5; 41.Nb6.** Inefficient, but the game is going to be a win in any case. 41.Ra5! cxb4; 42.Ncxe5 might well have forced resignation. **41... Nxb6; 42.Rxb6 c4; 43.Nc5 c3.**

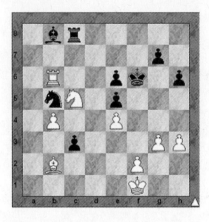

Smyslov **resigned** without waiting for Fischer to retreat the bishop to c1. Then the threat is not just at e6, but also a major fork at d7, hitting the king and bishop at b8.

**Game notes:** Vasily Smyslov was World Champion briefly in the 1950s, interrupting Botvinnik's reign. He remained a World Championship candidate until the mid-1980s, stopped in the final stage by Garry Kasparov. Since Americans couldn't travel to Cuba, this game was played by teletype from New York's Marshall Chess Club.

# GAME #16

# TWO KINGS ON THE RUN

**THE PLAYERS**
Bobby Fischer (White)
vs.
Nicolas Rossolimo (U.S.A.)

**THE LOCATION**
The United States Championship,
in New York, U.S.A.,
on 12/28/1965

## LESSON: THE KING IN THE CENTER BETTER HAVE GOOD RUNNING SHOES!

Although castling is recommended in the vast majority of games, there are a few openings where the king can stay in the center for a while. When the center is completely closed, and there is no way to get the blockading pawns out of the way, the king can maintain his temporary home.

Sooner or later, the defenses will develop cracks, and the king will have to flee. The terrain between the king and a safe harbor may be very exposed. In this case it will be hard to dodge the enemy bullets. An experienced player will often maintain an escape route of safe squares, but even then, the king has to be prepared to run. Any delay or wasted time can prove fatal.

The game below shows both kings in the center. Each must make a dash for the door, but only one succeeds. The value of having a good escape route is shown. So are the consequences of having one that only seems safe!

**1.e4 e6; 2.d4 d5; 3.Nc3 Nf6; 4.Bg5 Bb4.**

The opening is the MacCutcheon Variation of the French Defense. This is a cross between the Classical defense with …Nf6 and Winawer's plan with …Bb4. Once considered a surprise weapon, it is now a major branch of the French Defense.

**5.e5.** Since the knight is pinned and cannot move, Black's reply is forced. **5…h6; 6.Bd2.** The bishop can also retreat to e3. If it goes to h4, however, Black can play …g5, so the knight is unpinned in any case. **6…Bxc3; 7.bxc3.** This is the correct capture. White often allows the doubling of c-pawns in the French. The bishop would not accomplish anything sitting at c3. **7…Ne4; 8.Qg4.**

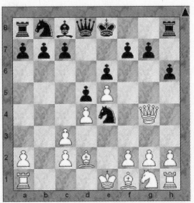

This move forces Black to choose between defending the g-pawn with the king and advancing it to g6. In the first case, Black cannot castle but is relatively safe at f8. If the pawn advances, the dark squares on the kingside become weak. White can then use the h-pawn to attack.

**8...g6.** This plan is seen much more frequently, though the king move is still seen around. Objectively, the strategies may have equal merit, but most chess players are uncomfortable giving up the right to castle. **9.Bd3.** This forces Black to give up the well-posted knight for the White bishop, but at the same time, White will find it more difficult to exploit Black's weak dark squares. **9...Nxd2; 10.Kxd2.**

White can't castle, but his king has plenty of defense. Black will try to crack open the fortress. **10...c5!; 11.Nf3 Nc6!** When Fischer wrote about this game back in 1969, opening experts preferred 11...Qc7. Now, the move played by Rossolimo is considered best by many. **12.Qf4.**

Since the dark square bishop is gone, White uses the queen to work the dark squares. Black is prevented from castling, as that would drop the pawn at h6.

**12...Qc7?!** Rossolimo sets up a little trick. The idea is to play ... f5, and if White captures using the en passant rule, then Black would capture White's queen. Remember, the en passant capture is available when the opponent advances a pawn two squares and it lands next to one of your pawns. You can then capture the enemy pawn with yours as if it had only moved one square. So if Black plays ...f5, White can capture with the pawn at e5, taking the enemy pawn at f6.

Rossolimo's move eliminates the capture, and the queen seems to put pressure on the center. Fischer thought she should go to a5 instead. 12...Qa5 pins White's pawn at c3, so a capture at d4 is threatened. He then recommended 13.Rab1, but Black has countered with 13...c4; 14.Be2 b5. White might try, for example 15.a3, hoping to lure the queen away from the pawn at b5. Then 15...Bd7 indirectly defends the pawn, because if a White rook every captures it, the knight can move away and do some damage while the Black bishop hungrily eyes the rook. So, in Golubev vs. Smikovsky, Moscow 1996, White shifted the rook back to a1 to defend the pawn. 12...Qe7 is a popular move, which has the benefit of maintaining surveillance of f6 while supporting the dark squares on the queenside. This is a bit defensive for Rossolimo, who just loved to attack.

**13.h4.** Fischer prepares to undermine the kingside. Afterwards, he thought that immediate infiltration was a better plan. 13.Qf6 Rg8; 14.h4 was his suggestion, and many years later it got a practical test in the game Jepson vs. Berebora, played in Hungary in 1990. 14...h5; 15.Rhb1 cxd4; 16.cxd4 Na5; 17.Ng5 put Black under considerable pressure.

**13...f5!** Fischer wrote that this move restores "parity." There is so much tension in the position that the game lies on a razor's edge. There is certainly nothing drawish about it! The first mistake will prove costly. A second will be fatal.

**14.g4!?** This adds another pressure point to the mix! Fischer is often at his most deadly when forces are under attack in multiple locations. Here there are contested squares at c5, d4, f5, g4 and potentially at g5 and h5. **14...cxd4; 15.cxd4 Ne7?** The first mistake.

Although the knight defends important kingside squares, Bobby needed a more active plan. 15...Bd7; 16.gxf5 gxf5; 17.Rhg1 O-O-O! would have completed Black's development. The king would be safe, and if Bobby played his intended 18.Rg6, where he claims the better prospects, Black could counter with 18...Qb6! and he might have found himself in a bit of trouble! **16.gxf5 exf5; 17.Bb5+.**

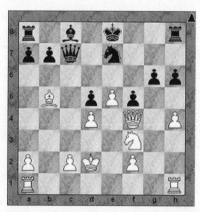

That's what you get when you leave your king in the center for too long! To preserve castling privilege, Black can either return the knight to c6 or block with the bishop. Instead, he not only gives up castling rights, but moves his king to the wrong square!

**17...Kf8?!** If the king had to move, it should have gone in the other direction. There is some hope of safety on the queenside. Still, Black's position is not beyond repair.

17...**Bd7**; 18.**Bxd7+ Qxd7**; 19.**e6!** is given by Fischer, but it does require some explanation. The idea is to sacrifice the pawn to clear the way for an attack on the e-file, while the Black king is still stuck in the center. 19...**Qxe6**; 20.**Rhe1 Qd7**; 21.**Qe5 Rh7**; does leave Black tied down, but Bobby may have been a bit optimistic, as there is no clear way to get to the enemy king and Black may be able to escape by castling.

17...**Kd8!**; 18.**Bd3 Be6** would have been tough to crack. Black can bring the rook to c8 and create some threats of his own.

**18.Bd3 Be6; 19.Ng1!** The knight temporarily retreats to g1, so that it can find a way to get to f4, once the queen moves away. The knight at f4 will put pressure on d5, e6, g6 and h5! **19...Kf7.** Here the king helps defend the pawn at g6, but that isn't a suitable task for a king! If the king were at d8, Black might eventually lose a pawn on the kingside, but in the meantime threats could be mounted against the White king. **20.Nh3 Rac8; 21.Rhg1.** More pressure at g6.

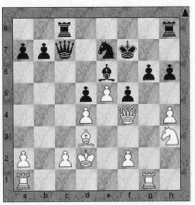

**21...b6.** The problem with this move is that it cuts off the path to a5, which is a checking square. This definitely limits Black's options. 21...Qc3+ also loses, according to Fischer, but Huebner has raised some interesting questions about the line he gave. 22.Ke3 Rc4, instead of 22...Nc6, looks about even. Black can later play ...b6, as the queen has an alternative path to a5 should she require one.

**22.h5 Qc3+; 23.Ke2.**

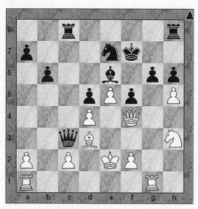

**23...Nc6?** This move abandons g6, which is a very bad idea with the king sitting at f7. The knight at e7 provided great defense, though it was just sitting there. Defending the pawn with the king in order to free the knight for other action was the strategic blunder of this game. Rossolimo wasn't fond of defense, and decided to go for activity at all costs.

23...Rcg8! was correct. once you have been forced to defend passively, you may as well go all the way. Trying to transform your position from passive defense to active counterplay is rarely possible because there are too many defensive needs that have to take priority. 24.hxg6+ and now 24...Nxg6; 25.Qf3 was left with no further comment by Fischer. The assumption is that the pawn at f5 will fall and the game will be over. Again, Huebner calls this into question with the simple 25...Qxd4 threatening to capture with check! Instead of moving the queen to f3, he finds a path to the advantage by capturing at g6 right away.

On the other hand, 24...Rxg6; 25.Qh4 brings a decisive advantage, according to Fischer. Huebner checked this out and offered the following supporting line, which contains an excellent example of an intermezzo: 25...Rhg8; 26.Rxg6 Rxg6; 27.Rg1 Rxg1; 28.Qf6+. Instead of recapturing at g1 right away, White uses an intermezzo to drive then enemy king back. After the capture at g1, Black will

be able to grab the d-pawn but then his king gets scissored. 28...
Ke8; 29.Nxg1 Qxd4?; 30.Bb5+ Kd8; 31.Qf8+ Kc7; 32.Qxe7+
and mate in seven!

**24.hxg6+ Kg7; 25.Rad1!** The finishing touch. Fischer sacrifices
the d-pawn but can now retreat the king to the home rank. This
was not possible with the rook under attack at a1, since the king
retreat would then cut off the defending rook at g1 and the rook
would fall with check.

**25...Nxd4+; 26.Kf1 Rhe8; 27.Rg3!** Precision to the end!
Rossolimo was not without resources, even in this position. Fischer
spotted the trick. 27.Qh4 threatens to invade at f6 but it allows
Black to get away with 27...Nf3!; 28.Qf6+ Kg8; 29.Bxf5 Nh2+!;
30.Kg2 Qf3+; 31.Kxh2 Qxf5 and Black has reasonable prospects
for survival. **27...Nc6.** How sad. The knight just keeps coming
back to this square, never accomplishing anything significant.
**28.Qh4 Nxe5.** White no longer has the check at f6, but there
are other problems. **29.Nf4! Ng4.** 29...Nxd3; 30.Rdxd3 Qa1+;
31.Kg2 and Nh5+ is coming. **30.Nxe6+ Rxe6; 31.Bxf5 Qc4+;
32.Kg1.** The White king has found safety in the kingside castle, so
Black, facing multiple shish-kebab on the c8-h3 diagonal, fourth
rank and g-file, **resigned.**

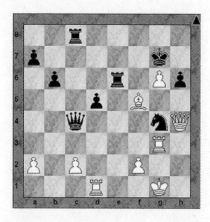

**Game notes:** Another United States Championship title is par for the course for Fischer. His opponent, Nicholas Rossolimo, was a player with a great love of attack. He created many brilliant masterpieces with creative displays. Unfortunately, his defensive skills were not on the same level as his offense.

# GAME #17

# SMASH THE MIRROR!

**THE PLAYERS**
Bobby Fischer (White)
vs.
Jacek Bednarski (Poland)

**THE LOCATION**
The Olympiad,
in Havana, Cuba,
on 10/30/1966

## LESSON: THE MAGIC POSITION

Every chess player has at least one magic position. A magic position is a position you have in your repertoire to play as both White and Black. After all, some opponents might choose to play the exact moves against you when you are in the same side of the board. The magic position requires a special psychological attitude. After all, as White you try to get to a position where you have some sort of tangible advantage over Black; you want to get to a position where the chances favor your side even more.

So the positions that you play from both sides of the board have to appear to slightly favor White, while seeming completely equal for Black! For many players, the magic position is usually evaluated and as unclear. With so many computers in use, however, it is hard to engage in this part of self-deception a rational level.

Some players aim for magic positions where White has a small and temporary advantage. The advantage won't have serious consequences in the endgame. A player with good endgame skills can easily defend inferior positions. Other players, including Fischer and Kasparov, search for new ideas so that they can crush their opposition, who are caught unprepared when faced with Fischer's novelties. The following game documents Fischer's skills.

**1.e4 c5; 2.Nf3 d6; 3.d4 cxd4; 4.Nxd4 Nf6; 5.Nc3 a6.**

Bednarski chooses Fischer's favorite Najdorf Variation of the Sicilian. But Bobby was to become equally famous for his own attack against it!

**6.Bc4 e6; 7.Bb3.** This is a plan originally worked out by Sozin and polished by Fischer. White places a lot of pressure at e6, and can later add to it by advancing the f-pawn. **7...Nbd7.** Putting the knight at d7 instead of c6 keeps the game within the confines of the Najdorf Variation. The knight often heads to c5.

**8.f4.** In the Najdorf Sicilian, White's king frequents the queenside, so that the kingside pawns can be advanced without exposing the king to attack. Of course Black will aim all weapons at the queenside. An exciting battle is almost certain. **8...Nc5; 9.f5.**

**9...Nfxe4?** Bednarski chooses a variation which did not have a bad reputation. Until this game! Fischer takes apart Black's position with surgical precision, unafraid of Bednarski's home preparation. Black has sensible alternatives, including capturing the bishop at b3 and attacking the central knight with ...e5. **10.fxe6! Qh4+.** Black was counting on the kingside attack, but Fischer dismisses it effortlessly. 10...fxe6; 11.Nxe4 Nxe4; 12.O-O Qe7 was the line Fischer proposed, but it still hasn't seen action. **11.g3 Nxg3.**

The position seems menacing. The knight can't be captured because the h-pawn is pinned. Yet if it is not captured, it will move away with discovered check, possibly grabbing a rook along the way.

**12.Nf3!** First, Bobby eliminates the discovered checks by chasing away the enemy queen. **12...Qh5; 13.exf7+.** Now the attack is in Fischer's hands, and he doesn't let go until they are firmly around the enemy king's neck. **13...Kd8; 14.Rg1!** Fischer unpins the h-pawn while attacking the knight with the rook as well. **14...Nf5; 15.Nd5 Qxf7.**

The queen eliminates the advanced pawn but walks into a deadly pin. Black's king has no where to hide and castling is no longer possible. It is just a matter of time before the walls cave in. **16.Bg5+ Ke8; 17.Qe2+ Be6; 18.Nf4.** The pins on the e-file and a2-g8 diagonal are just too much. Now the king will have to move up to defend the bishop.

**18...Kd7; 19.O-O-O Qe8; 20.Bxe6+ Nxe6; 21.Qe4!** The queen creates threats at b7, e6 and f5. **21...g6; 22.Nxe6.**

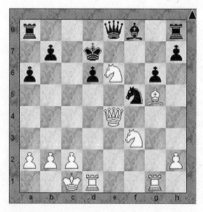

Black **resigned.** If the knight is captured then Fischer grabs the b-pawn with check and brings a rook to e1 to finish things off.

**Game notes:** For this world team championship, Fischer and the other Americans were allowed to travel to Cuba. Bobby responded with a magnificent performance, scoring fifteen points in seventeen games! The team finished in second place behind the perennial winning team from the Soviet Union. A fantastic result!

# GAME #18

# BISHOPS SWEEP THE BOARD!

**THE PLAYERS**
Bobby Fischer (White)
vs.
Leonid Stein (U.S.S.R)

**THE LOCATION**
The Interzonal,
in Sousse, Tunisia
on 10/24/1967

## LESSON: BISHOPS CAN BE EFFECTIVE FROM A DISTANCE

It is often said that bishops are better than knights, but the situation is often complicated. The advantage of the bishop over the knight is that the bishop can travel great distances in one move whereas the knight's scope is severely limited.

When there are open lines for bishops, they can sweep the board, zoning in on targets quickly while working from a safe distance. Often the bishops operate from a fianchetto position as, for example, in the dragon variation of the Sicilian Defense for the King's Indian Defense. They can even be effective when sitting on their home squares!

In the Spanish game, the bishops often do very little early in the game. The light square bishop often sits at c2, its vision blocked by the pawn at e4, until, in the middle game, the pawn somehow gets out of the way and the full force of the bishop is applied to the enemy kingside. In the following game, Fischer uses bishops stationed at b1 and c1, while his opponent has one useful bishop placed on a long diagonal at b7.

**1.e4 e5; 2.Nf3 Nc6; 3.Bb5 a6; 4.Ba4 Nf6; 5.O-O Be7; 6.Re1 b5; 7.Bb3 d6; 8.c3 O-O; 9.h3.**

This is the standard position of the Spanish Inquisition. White keeps the enemy bishop off of g4, so that the knight at f3 will not be pinned. This means that the coming advance to d4 will have plenty of support.

**9...Bb7.** This move came as a bit of a surprise, since it was, at the time, a very rare continuation. Then, moving the knight to a5 immediately, the traditional plan developed by Mikhail Chigorin was still the main line. However, Stein had played the White side of the line the previous year, and there were well known encounters between Grandmasters that enabled both players to be somewhat familiar with it. Eventually, Black's plan with ...Bb7 paired with ... Re8 would become the main line.

**10.d4 Na5.** Moving the rook to e8 is the modern handling of the position. Black has also tried ...Qd7 here. **11.Bc2 Nc4.** This plan has the knight hopping all over the board. In fact, Black has developed more pieces than White, and the loss of time transferring the knight, eventually to d7, is not significant. Given Black's intentions, however, it would have been easier to use Gyula Breyer's plan (9...Nb8) and get the knight there directly. At the time, the plan used in this game was undergoing a number of tests, and White had not been particularly successful against it.

**12.b3 Nb6; 13.Nbd2 Nbd7.**

Black's position makes a solid impression. The basic strategy is to play ...c5, perhaps after putting a rook at c8. Fischer decides to discourage that plan. 13...exd4; 14.cxd4 c5 was recommended by Fischer as a more active plan.

**14.b4!** This move creates a backward pawn at c4, but Fischer plans to eliminate it by advancing to c4 after moving his bishop to b2. **14...exd4; 15.cxd4.** Black has given up the central pawn that anchored his center, and allows Fischer to establish the ideal pawn center with pawns at e4 and d4. Stein could have, and should have, challenged this center immediately by advancing his pawn to c5.

**15...a5.** The pawn at b4 is deflected by a temporary pawn sacrifice. Still, this was perhaps not the best plan for Black. 15...c5; 16.bxc5 dxc5; 17.d5 was dismissed by Fischer claiming that "White's steamroller in the center is more formidable than Black's queenside majority." Many years later, this evaluation was tested. 17...Re8; 18.Nf1 Bd6; 19.Ng3. There doesn't seem to be anything better, though we don't have analysis from Fischer or other Grandmasters to help evaluate the position. 19...Bxg3; 20.fxg3 c4; 21.Kh2 Rc8 gave Black a strong queenside initiative in a correspondence game, Hoszowski vs. Cimicki, 1993.

**16.bxa5 c5!** 16...Rxa5 is not appropriate because of 17.d5 c5; 18.dxc6 Bxc6; 19.Nd4 with a dominating position for White.

**17.e5!** Fischer improves on the simple fianchetto of the bishop, seen in Ciric vs. Robatsch, from the same year. **17...dxe5.** 17... Ne8!? looks passive but the idea is to actively confront White's central pawns. The great pawn structure theoretician Hans Kmoch wondered whether Black might run into trouble on the queenside, where the b-pawn is weak and White's pawn at a5 might not be removed. 18.exd6 Bxd6; 19.Ne4 gives White a clear initiative, without the counterplay that Black is able to achieve in the game.

**18.dxe5 Nd5.** Now Black's other knight gets to go on a bit of a journey. **19.Ne4 Nb4!** Black must play as actively as possible on the queenside. Although White's kingside attack is not yet underway, you can see the storm clouds gathering. The knights have central positions not far from the enemy king. White's Spanish bishop at c2 aims at h7. The dark square bishop is ready to deploy and the rook at e1 can be lifted to the third rank and transferred to the g-file. Black cannot sit back and watch while the attack develops.

**20.Bb1 Rxa5.** Black has recovered the pawn and has pressure at a2. If the a-pawn falls, White will find it difficult to stop the advancing Black pawns. On the other hand, all this is taking place in the distant regions of the queenside, and Fischer isn't really concerned with that part of the board. **21.Qe2!**

**21...Nb6?** This is one knight move too many. It was time for Stein to start thinking about the kingside. 21...Re8! was the correct move. The knight, instead of wandering to the queenside, could have been tucked away at f8 to defend the critical h7 square. Fischer acknowledged that after this move he would not have had any advantage.

Would Fischer even have had equality? 22.e6 is an attempt, but Fischer pointed out that Black can defend with 22...fxe6; 23.Neg5 Bxg5; 24.Nxg5 Nf8; 25.Qh5 g6.

According to Fischer 22.Rd1 is countered by 22...Qc7, but 23.Neg5 is not refuted by 23...Bxg5?!; 24.Nxg5 Nxe5; 25.Bxh7+ Kf8 as some have thought because 26.Qh5 Rxa2; 27.Rxa2 Nxa2; 28.Bb2 gives White an overwhelming attack. Instead of the capture at g5, 23...Nf8! is correct. Then 24.Bb2 h6; 25.Ne4 Nd5 demonstrates the correct use of the knights. I think that White has less than nothing in this position, and Black has all the winning chances.

**22.Nfg5.**

White's knights and long-range bishops are poised for the kill. Black's forces are merely offside. The knights on the b-file would require many moves to reposition themselves for defense of the kingside. White's bishops at c1 and b1, on the other hand, are ready to take an active role in the battle. **22...Bxe4!?**

Fischer claimed that this was the only move to keep Black in the game. He showed that 22...h6; 23.Nh7! is crushing. For example, 23...Kxh7?; 24.Nxc5+ Kg8; 25.Nxb7 forks the queen and rook. If Black tries 23...Re8 instead of capturing the bishop, White has 24.Nhf6+! Here 24...gxf6 leads to a pretty checkmate: 25.Qg4+ Kh8; 26.Nd6! Bxd6; 27.Qf5 Kg7; 28.Bxh6+ Kxh6; 29.Qh7+ Kg5; 30.f4+ Kxf4; 31.Qh4. Checkmate. Or 24...Bxf6; 25.Nxf6+ gxf6; 26.Qg4+ Kf8; 27.Bxh6+ Ke7. Here White doesn't play the "obvious" discovered check by capturing at f6, but instead prepares to play e6, after taking away d6 as a flight square with 28.Bf4! Black could try capturing at f6 with the queen instead of the bishop.

Instead of capturing White's knight with the pawn 25...Qxf6 looks like a nice trick, because the queen cannot be captured thanks to the pin on the e-file, but counting pieces reveals that after 26.exf6 Rxe2; 27.Rxe2, Black is down the exchange with checkmate threatened on the back rank.

Black can try a different defense, instead of advancing the h-pawn as in the sideline we just looked at. It isn't so clear that 22...g6 gets ripped apart by 23.e6! f5; 24.Nf7! where Fischer notes that White plans Bb2 "with a crushing attack." Still, after 24...Qd5; 25.Bb2 Rfa8! it is hard to see anything special for White. **23.Qxe4.**

**23...g6; 24.Qh4 h5; 25.Qg3!** Fischer has provoked weaknesses in the Black defensive formation and is ready to unleash tricks at e6. **25...Nc4!** 25...Bxg5; 26.Bxg5 Qd4; 27.Bf6! leads to destruction on the dark squares. Black can't take the rook. 27...Qxa1? is demolished by the beautiful 28.Bxg6! Qxe1+; 29.Kh2 and it is mate in four.

**26.Nf3?!** This is an inaccurate move order. Fischer attributes this to a power failure that knocked out the lights as he was considering his move. Fischer should have pushed the e-pawn right away! 26.e6! f5; 27.Nf3 was correct. He gives the following line: 27...Kg7 (27... Rf6?; 28.Bg5 Kh7; 29.Bxf6 Bxf6 looks like it regains the exchange down at a1, but White has a trick. 30.Bxf5! gxf5; 31.Rad1 followed by Rd7+.) 28.Qf4 Rf6. Fischer points out that after ...Rh8, play would transpose to the game, without allowing Stein to adopt the defense that he overlooks in his reply.

**26...Kg7?** 26...Nd3! was the move Stein missed but this would really have thrown a monkey wrench into Fischer's plans. Fischer said he was worrying about this during the power failure, after he made his move. He would have to avoid 27.Rd1? Nxc1; 28.Rxd8 Ne2+; 29.Kh2 Rxd8! and White's queen remains trapped! Fischer's comment that "White has nothing" after Black captures at c1 is quite an understatement. In fact, White loses in this line. However, he might have seen 27.Bxd3! Qxd3; 28.Bg5, which was what Fischer eventually came up with. There is a lot of pressure on the dark squares, for example 28...Re8; 29.Bxe7 Rxe7; 30.Qg5 Re6; 31.Rad1 Qf5; 32.Qh6!

**27.Qf4 Rh8!**

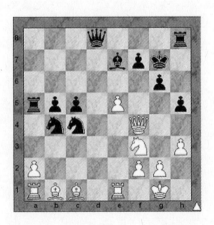

A good defensive strategy. Black just needs one or two moves to eliminate any danger of White pushing the pawn to e6. The other rook can drop back to a6 and the queen can come to d7. Fischer realizes that he must strike immediately!

**28.e6! f5?** A poor choice, because White's passed pawn is too strong. There was a much better plan available. 28...Bf6! was correct. White would have a tough time winning, according to Fischer, who provided the following analysis. 29.exf7 Bxa1 and now:

30.f8=Q+ Qxf8; 31.Qc7+ Kg8; 32.Bxg6 Nd5; 33.Qb7 Nf6; 34.Bf4 Rh7!, meeting the threat of Ng5 followed by Bf7+. 35.Bxh7+ Nxh7; 36.Qd5+ Qf7; 37.Qxf7+ Kxf7; 38.Rxa1 where White has an extra pawn and the advantage of a bishop against a knight, but the a-pawn is weak and Black has a strong passed c-pawn.

Instead of promoting the pawn, White could play 30.Re8 Rxe8; 31.Qh6+ since 31...Kxf7; 32.Qxg6+ Ke7; 33.Bg5+ Kd7 leaves the Black king exposed and wins the queen, but after 34.Bxd8 Rxd8 Black has two rooks and a knight for queen and pawn. White can pick off a weak pawn or two, but doesn't have enough force to win in the middlegame. **29.Bxf5!**

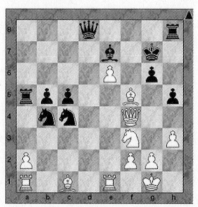

A demolition sacrifice that must be declined. **29...Qf8!** 29...Bd6 gets busted by 30.e7! and 29...gxf5; 30.Qg3+ Kh7; 31.Ng5+ Bxg5; 32.Bxg5 Qd3 tries to get queens off but 33.Qc7+ Kg6; 34.Qf7+!

Kxg5; 35.Qg7+ Kf4; 36.Qxh8 is a killer. Although material is even, Black can resign. The immediate threat is Qh6. Checkmate.

Black can try moving the king to f8, instead of h7, but there is no relief there, either: 30...Kf8; 31.Qg6 Qe8; 32.Bh6+ Rxh6; 33.Qxh6+ Kg8; 34.Ng5 Bxg5; 35.Qxg5+ Kh7; 36.Rad1 and Black has no defense.

**30.Be4?!** There was a better way, pointed out by the British master Paul Littlewood. Fischer's move is good enough, however. 30.Nh4! would have been more effective. Black still can't eat the piece without suffering indigestion. 30...Bxh4; 31.Qxh4 Qxf5; 32.Qe7+ Kg8; 33.Qd8+ Kg7; 34.Qc7+ Kg8; 35.e7 and the passed pawn has a clear path to its promotion. **30...Qxf4; 31.Bxf4.**

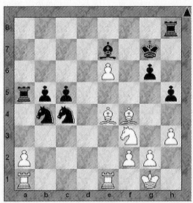

Swapping queens leads to a complicated endgame. Where there are complications, there are ways to go wrong! **31...Re8?** The bold capture 31...Rxa2! offers the best chance of survival. 32.Rxa2 Nxa2; 33.Ne5 looks strong, because the knight at e5 can't safely be captured. But Black has a surprising resource. 33...g5!; 34.Bg3 Nb4; 35.Nxc4 bxc4; 36.Be5+ Bf6; 37.Bd6 Re8; 38.Bxc5 Nd3; 39.Bxd3 cxd3 is clearly better for White, but not at all easy to win.

**32.Rad1 Ra6; 33.Rd7.** Occupying the seventh rank usually proves deadly, and it is a good enough plan, though Fischer could have been a bit more precise. 33.Bb7 Ra7; 34.Rd7 would have been more efficient. **33...Rxe6; 34.Ng5 Rf6; 35.Bf3! Rxf4.** Black has nothing better than to give up the exchange. **36.Ne6+ Kf6; 37.Nxf4 Ne5; 38.Rb7 Bd6; 39.Kf1 Nc2; 40.Re4 Nd4; 41.Rb6 Rd8; 42.Nd5+ Kf5.** The game was adjourned here, and Fischer finished it off effectively when it was resumed.

**43.Ne3+ Ke6; 44.Be2 Kd7; 45.Bxb5+ Nxb5; 46.Rxb5 Kc6; 47.a4 Bc7; 48.Ke2 g5; 49.g3 Ra8; 50.Rb2 Rf8; 51.f4 gxf4; 52.gxf4 Nf7; 53.Re6+ Nd6; 54.f5 Ra8; 55.Rd2 Rxa4; 56.f6.**

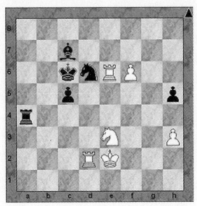

Black **resigned** before Fischer could plant the knight at d5, preventing the Black rook from coming to f4 and preventing the advance of the f-pawn.

**Game notes:** The scandal at the 1967 Interzonal, the official qualifier for the World Championship competitions, is a long and complex tale. Fischer withdrew from the tournament when his specific requests (or demands) regarding playing conditions weren't met. He had played ten games, but forfeited the ninth and tenth, won in rounds eleven and twelve against his countrymen Reshevsky and Byrne. Fischer forfeited the last round against Larsen, who won the tournament.

# GAME #19

# THE WANDERING ROOK

## THE PLAYERS
Bobby Fischer (White)
vs.
Anthony Saidy (U.S.A.)

## THE LOCATION
The Metropolitan Chess League,
in New York U.S.A.,
on 1/1/1969

## LESSON: YOU CAN PLACE YOUR FORCES IN DANGER AS LONG AS THERE IS A WAY OUT

It isn't just the king that needs defense. Sometimes you send forces into dangerous territory, with no clear way back. You must be very careful about sending a piece to attack, especially all by itself. After all, the hunter can soon become the hunted!

Many beginners bring a rook into the game by advancing the pawn in front of its two squares, sneaking the rook up the file and then sliding over to a useful position. This is known as a "rook lift." The rook lift rarely works early in the game. Often there is an enemy bishop taking aim at the square the rook will use as a transfer point.

If you try to use a rook deep inside enemy territory, you have to be very careful that it does not become trapped. A trapped piece will often wind up as an enemy prisoner, and is usually executed. Make sure that if you send forces into the danger zone, they have some method of escape!

**1.c4 e5.** Bobby didn't mind being a tempo down in the Sicilian Defense (1.e4 c5). This is known as the King's English, and is the boldest and sharpest reply to the English. **2.Nc3 Nc6; 3.g3 f5.**

Another aggressive choice. We now have a reversed form of the Grand Prix Attack (1.e4 c5 2.Nc3 Nc6; 3.f4), but Black has control of the d4-square, so the liberating move d4 isn't achieved immediately. **4.Bg2 Nf6; 5.e3 Bc5; 6.d3 f4.** The temporary sacrifice of the f-pawn is a standard part of the Grand Prix strategy, but a tempo down, it is a bit optimistic. **7.exf4 O-O; 8.Nge2.**

Although this move has been subject to criticism, it has been seen in most of the games played to this position. Modern authorities consider it a good move and believe that Black cannot achieve full equality from the position!

**8...Qe8; 9.O-O d6; 10.Na4 Bd4; 11.Nxd4.** 11.fxe5! is the right move, according to Saidy. No one has taken up his suggestion, which has been a secret for over three decades! 11...Bg4 is a reasonable reply, but then White might consider capturing at c6 followed by Qc2. **11...exd4; 12.h3 h5!?**

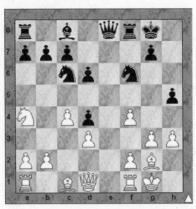

A risky move, but White was establishing a strong kingside attack, so Fischer had to do something to discourage a pawn advance to g4. Since that is what Bobby was out to prevent, Saidy should have tried to achieve it somehow.

**13.a3 a5.** Once again, Fischer thwarts White's plans. The pawn will not get to b4 quickly. **14.b3 Qg6; 15.Nb2 Bf5.**

Black's pieces operate effectively on the kingside and put pressure on d3, but White has plenty of defense. In the long run, his bishop pair should prove to be an advantage. 16.Qc2. 16.Re1 might have been tried. **16...Nd7; 17.Re1 Nc5; 18.Bf1.** White's position is unpleasantly passive. The bishops are no better than the knights. **18...Ra6!?** Fischer decides that the rook will play a role at b6. It will eat the pawn at b3! **19.Bd2 Rb6; 20.Bxa5 Rxb3.**

**21.Bd2.** 21.Bb4 Nxb4; 22.axb4 Rxb4; 23.Ra3 might have been considered. White gives back the pawn, but takes control of the a-file.

**21...Ra8; 22.a4 Ra6; 23.a5 Kh7.** 23...Nb4; 24.Bxb4 Rxb4; 25.Ra3 brought White a small advantage in Karpov vs. Bellon, 1973. So clearly Karpov agreed with Saidy's strategy!

**24.Red1.** White is managing to defend all the weaknesses, but it's under great pressure. Fischer decides to concentrate on the queenside. **24...b6!?; 25.Be1 bxa5; 26.Na4!** White's pawn sacrifice is followed by a blockade of the e-pawn. The pawn at d3 must fall too, but by releasing all the tension, Saidy gains freedom to maneuver. This was probably the best decision, though it clearly concedes the advantage to Fischer. **26...Rxd3; 27.Bxd3 Bxd3; 28.Qa2!**

The idea is that an exchange of knights will bring the queen to c4, where she defends the pawn at c4 and puts pressure on the light squares.

**28...Nb4.** 28...Nxa4 would surely have been countered by the exchange sacrifice 29.Rxd3! Qxd3; 30.Qxa4 with excellent drawing chances. 29.Qa3? This is where the game goes down the tubes. 29.Qb2! Nxa4; 30.Rxa4 Bc2 looks very impressive but after 31.Rxa5! Rxa5; 32.Bxb4 Bxd1; 33.Bxa5, the bishops of opposite colors would hold the draw, unless Fischer managed to invade the kingside.

**29...Nc2!; 30.Qb2 Nxa1; 31.Rxa1 Nxa4; 32.Rxa4.** If White had chosen correctly at move 29, this position would already have the rooks and a-pawn off the board! **32...Qe4!** A powerful centralizing move, which dooms White to defeat. **33.Bxa5?** Walking into a little combination, but the game was already beyond repair. **33...Rxa5!** Fischer uses an exchange sacrifice to deflect the rook from the home rank. **34.Rxa5 Qe1+; 35.Kh2 Qxa5; 36.Qxd4.** White **resigned**.

Black has an extra bishop and a safe king, so there is no point in continuing. Black would play 36…Qd2, followed by …Qc2 and the c-pawn falls.

**Game notes:** This was the only recorded game Bobby played in 1969, but it is very interesting. It was honored as the runner-up in the Chess Informant vote for the best game of the first half of 1969. Some of the notes above are based on personal communications from Tony Saidy, who pointed out several mistakes made by previous commentators.

# GAME #20  READY, AIM, FIRE!

### THE PLAYERS
Bobby Fischer (White)
vs.
William Addison (U.S.A.)

### THE LOCATION
The Interzonal,
in Palma de Majorca, Spain,
on 11/11/1970

## LESSON: AIM YOUR HEAVY ARTILLERY AT THE ENEMY KING AND QUEEN

When you are starting out in chess, it is sometimes good enough just to aim one of your pieces at an unprotected enemy piece, hoping your opponent won't notice. Indeed, many games are won or lost that way.

As you improve and face tougher opposition, it takes more than just an undisguised attack to pick off enemy pieces. You need to lay the groundwork by setting up your pieces in positions where they can strike quickly, even if there is no obvious attack.

There is a technique that can help set up possibilities to capture your opponent's forces. It is similar to man-on-man coverage in such sports as football and basketball. You can have your big guns track the enemy king and queen. You can aim your rook or queen at the opposing king, or target the enemy queen with your rook. Just sit on the same file, no matter how many pieces are in the way.

When opportunity arises, get the intervening pieces out of the way, somehow. Then many tactical tricks can appear as if by magic. If you are defending, avoid them by moving your king or queen out of the range of the enemy tracker.

**1.e4 d5.**

This is the Scandanavian Defense, where Black immediately confronts White's central pawn. The Scandinavian Defense was considered quite unusual at the time. Only in the 1990s did it achieve respectability. Black allows White keep a small initiative by capturing. **2.exd5 Qxd5.** Black can also play 2...Nf6 and recover the pawn later. That strategy is known as the Modern Variation. **3.Nc3 Qd8.** This is considered inferior to 3...Qa5 and 3...Qd6. Fischer is happy to have the lead in development!

**4.d4.** This move allows Fischer to occupy and control important central squares. The move also releases the bishop at c1, which can quickly enter the game. **4...Nf6; 5.Bc4 Bf5; 6.Qf3!** White attacks both the bishop at f5 and the pawn at b7. Often, an early move of the light square bishop will leave the b-pawn vulnerable to a White attack.

**6...Qc8.** Black defends against both threats. **7.Bg5!?** White offers the pawn at c2 for free. But while Black is grabbing the pawn, White just continues to bring his forces into attacking positions. **7...Bxc2; 8.Rc1.**

Notice how the rook at c1 aims at the enemy queen at c8. Although there are many pieces in the way, it is still something to worry about. **8...Bg6; 9.Nge2.** No tricks yet; there are still development tasks. **9...Nbd7; 10.O-O.** White has completed development, as the rooks are in view of each other and castling has been achieved. Black, on the other hand, needs at least five moves to complete his development. Although Fischer is down a pawn, there is more than enough compensation.

**10...e6.** Somehow, the bishop has to get out so that Black can castle. **11.Bxf6 gxf6; 12.d5!** Fischer tries to rip open the e-file. **12...e5.** Addison declines the invitation and takes a bit more of the center. **13.Bb5!**

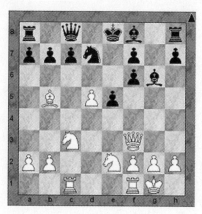

The pin against the knight at d7 is strong. White controls the c6-square with pawn, bishop and queen, so the pressure is hard to relieve. **13...Be7; 14.Ng3.** The f5-square, weakened by the ...e5 advance, is now firmly under control.

**14...a6; 15.Bd3.** Black's remaining defender of f5 is challenged. If it can be eliminated, the knight will have a wonderful home there. **15...Qd8.** The queen has traveled to d5 (now occupied by a White pawn) and back. Then to c8 and back. Not exactly productive play!

**16.h4.** Addison was hoping that Fischer would capture at g6, allowing Black to choose between undoubting the pawns or opening up the h-file. Instead, Fischer chooses to force the issue. **16...h5.** A major victory for Fischer. The Black h-pawn will be a great target in any endgame. **17.Bf5!** The idea is to bring a knight to e4. Then Black has to worry about the safety of the f-pawn, even though it is defended by three pieces. **17...Nb6.** Since the knight can't really defend f6, because it can be eliminated by White's bishop, Addison sends it off on other errands. **18.Nce4!** Fischer sacrifices the powerful pawn at d5, but gains a tremendous pin in return.

**18...Nxd5; 19.Rfd1.** Black's position is under pressure all over the place. White's pieces are perfectly placed, and not a single one of Black's is comfortable. **19...c6.** Pretty much forced. The threat was 20.Rxd5! Qxd5, and now the crushing blows rain down. 21.Nxf6+!! Bxe7; 22.Qxd5. **20.Nc3 Qb6.**

Notice that the Black queen and bishop would be forked if it were a White knight instead of a Black knight at d5. **21.Rxd5!** Fischer's exchange sacrifice achieves the goal! **21...cxd5; 22.Nxd5 Qxb2.** Yet another pawn is sacrificed. But Black hasn't yet castled or developed a rook, and the finish is brutal. **23.Rb1 Qxa2.** The queen has traveled far several times to grab a pawn for a snack, and Black has three extra pawns plus the exchange. That's almost a whole rook in value! It doesn't matter though, the king is a sitting duck. **24.Rxb7.**

Addison had seen enough and **gave up.** There are threats of Rxe7+ and Nc7+ followed by Nxa8. In addition, White has Bxg6 followed by Nxf6+.

**Game notes:** This game, played in a qualification stage for his eventual World Championship, shows Fischer in dominating form. He won the tournament, winning fifteen, drawing seven, and losing only once. It was to be his final tournament performance. After this event, he played only individual matches.

# THE BREAKS OF THE GAME!

**THE PLAYERS**

Bobby Fischer (White)

vs.

Tigran Petrosian (U.S.S.R.)

**THE LOCATION**

The Final Candidates Match,

at Buenos Aires, Argentina,

on 10/19/1971

## LESSON: THE PAWN STRUCTURE HAS A LONG-TERM EFFECT ON THE GAME

In a real army invasion, soldiers are well aware of the territory they invade, especially permanent features such as mountains and rivers. In chess, the pawn structure determines where the forces can go. Weaknesses in the pawn structure can last a long time. Some are even permanent.

Often a small weakness is acceptable when there are other factors that compensate. For example, an "isolated d-pawn," where there is a pawn at d4 or d5 (for White) and there is no friendly pawn on either the c-file or e-file. The isolated pawn has to be protected by other pieces. It is weak. At the same time, however, the pawn can be a real annoyance to the opponent, because it controls important squares in the enemy position. In addition, bishops usually have a great deal of mobility in such positions.

Some players even feel that an isolated d-pawn is, all things considered, a benefit. The great Siegbert Tarrasch felt strongly about this and developed a whole opening system for Black around it. I must admit, I'm a big fan.

Still, those benefits vanish in the endgame, where the weak pawn can often be captured without difficulty, unless the opponent is willing to commit the entire army to its defense. To advance in chess, you must learn when the isolated pawn is strong, and when it is weak.

**1.e4 c5; 2.Nf3 e6; 3.d4 cxd4; 4.Nxd4 a6.**

This is the Kan Variation of the Sicilian Defense. Black guards all of the squares that the White knight might use to invade Black's position. This weakens the dark squares a bit, but Black can control those with the queen and bishop. Black can try to activate the light square bishop at b7, after advancing the b-pawn one or two squares. In this game, however, Black heads for the territory of the Paulsen Variation.

**5.Bd3.** The standard move, preparing for castling. White will put a pawn at c4, to battle for the center, before bringing out the other knight. **5...Nc6.** Not too popular anymore. Black can play more aggressively by using the dark square bishop to attack the White knight. The most common defense, however, is the simple development of the knight at f6. **6.Nxc6 bxc6.** Petrosian chose to recapture with the b-pawn because the d-pawn is destined for d5, a common theme in the Sicilian. **7.O-O d5.**

Black plays the typical "Sicilian Break." The pawn at d5 challenges White's center. White's pawn at e4 can advance or capture, but Fischer adds fuel to the fire by aiming another pawn at d5.

**8.c4!? Nf6; 9.cxd5 cxd5; 10.exd5.** White is carving up the center, and Black has to choose whether or not to accept an Isolated pawn. Normally, Black captures with the knight. Sometimes the queen is used. Rarely, however, does Black capture with the pawn and leave it stranded in the center. Petrosian accepts the challenge.

**10...exd5.** Clearly the isolated d-pawn is going to play a significant role in the game. Part of White's strategy will be to dominate the neighboring files, so that the pawn is even more cut off from support even more. **11.Nc3! Be7; 12.Qa4+!**

**12...Qd7.** 12...Bd7! would have been the correct way to block the check. White has a small advantage, because Black's isolated d-pawn is weak. **13.Re1!** Fischer doesn't engage in cheap theatrics: 13.Bb5?! is very tempting, because if the bishop is captured, then the Black rook at a8 will be captured by the White queen. The a-pawn is pinned. But Black gets compensation after castling. For example, 13...axb5!; 14.Qxa8 O-O, the follow up with Bb7, and an eventual advance of the d-pawn will give Black an excellent game. 15.Bg5 Bb7; 16.Qa7 d4; 17.Rad1 Qg4! **13...Qxa4; 14.Nxa4.**

The isolated pawn is even weaker in the endgame, and White is halfway toward achieving his goal of dominating the c- and e-files. The pawn at a6, defended doubly for the moment, is also a potential weakness. Often, White has the luxury of a knight sitting at d4, blockading the pawn. That's an ideal situation, but Bobby can't achieve that. There is a potential fork at b6, but Petrosian renders it harmless.

**14...Be6; 15.Be3 O-O.** 15...Nd7 would have led to the following moves, according to Petrosian: 16.f4 g6; 17.Bd4 O-O; 18.Rac1 and White dominates most of the board.

**16.Bc5!** This is the key move. With the dark-squared bishops off the board, the rooks can attack the isolated pawn from the side. In addition, the c5-square will be more easily secured for occupation by the knight. 16.Nc5 could be played right away, but Black has a5! 17.Bd4 Bxc5; 18.Bxc5 Rfc8 with the initiative. **16...Rfe8; 17.Bxe7 Rxe7; 18.b4!**

Now you can really appreciate the weakness of the pawn at a6, which will come under the watchful eye of the knight from its new outpost at c5. This, combined with the power of the Be2, will tie down Black's forces.

**18...Kf8; 19.Nc5 Bc8.** Mission accomplished. Now Fischer must find a way to increase the pressure on d5 but how can he do this? **20.f3!** Fischer's plan is almost brutal in its simplicity; he threatens to exchange rooks, march his king up the diagonal to d4, chase the knight from f6 and grab the weak pawn at d5.

**20...Rea7?** Though this move was roundly criticized, Black was in trouble anyway. Proposing an exchange of knights, as recommended by the endgame specialist Yuri Averbakh, was most likely the best of a bad bunch of options, **21.Re5!** Just as planned way back at move 13! **21...Bd7.**

**22.Nxd7+!!** The knight, though well placed, has done its job and now the domination of the remaining open file is the primary objective. White will now enjoy the advantage of bishop over knight in the endgame. The longer reach of the bishop, especially in a wide open position like this, is very useful. When it can take aim at an isolated d-pawn, it's even better.

**22...Rxd7; 23.Rc1.** Fischer is planning to use c6 as an invasion square. The weakness of the pawns continues to plague Black. **23...Rd6.** Black's rook will be used to defend several weak pawns, but that means it isn't available for other uses. This is a very typical problem in an endgame with an isolated d-pawn.

**24.Rc7.** The sixth is protected — but the seventh rank is now available. Black quickly runs out of moves. **24...Nd7; 25.Re2 g6; 26.Kf2 h5.** 26...Rb8; 27.a3 a5; 28.b5 a4 might have provided some counterplay, according to World Champion Mikhail Botvinnik. Still, Black's knight is no match for White's bishop, and Black's weak pawns are easier to get at.

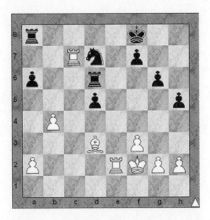

**27.f4!** A precise move that further limits Black's options. 27.Ke3 would have allowed Black's knight back into the game with 27... Ne5. **27...h4.** 27...Nb6; 28.Ree7 Rf6 was suggested by World Champion Tigran Petrosian. After 29.g3 The domination of the seventh rank and blockade of the isolated d-pawn give White a clear advantage. **28.Kf3 f5.**

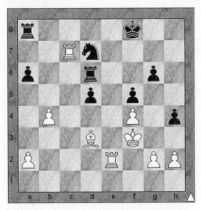

**29.Ke3.** Black is virtually in zugzwang, so he advances his prized pawn, and opens up more lines for White. **29...d4+.** 29...Nf6 loses to 30.Kd4 Ne4; 31.Rec2 when the c-file is just as important as the 7th rank. White's queenside pawn majority is mobile, while the Black pawn at d5 is going nowhere.

**30.Kd2 Nb6; 31.Ree7 Nd5; 32.Rf7+ Ke8; 33.Rb7.** This appears to drop a pawn, but in fact it guarantees victory. **33... Nxb4; 34.Bc4!**

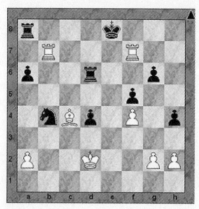

Petrosian **resigned**, because 34...Nc6; 35.Rh7 Rf6 loses to 36.Rh8+ Rf8; 37.Bf7+.

**Game notes:** Former World Champion Tigran Petrosian was Fischer's last barrier to a title match. Although he didn't pitch a shutout, he won the match convincingly. Petrosian defeated Botvinnik in 1963 to put a final end to Botvinnik's off-and-on ownership of the title since 1948. He held it for just three years, losing it to Boris Spassky. And Spassky, of course, was Fischer's next opponent.

# ENEMY PAWNS CAN BE PROVOKED

**THE PLAYERS**
Bobby Fischer (White)
vs.
Boris Spassky (U.S.S.R.)

**THE LOCATION**
The World Championship Match,
at Reykjavik, Iceland,
on 7/23/1972

## LESSON: THE PAWN STRUCTURE CAN REVEAL WHICH PIECES SHOULD BE EXCHANGED TO REACH AN OPTIMAL ENDGAME

You've already seen the importance of pawn structure and the endgame. Putting these two together can provide guidance in another of chess's most difficult tasks. As you enter the endgame, you must decide which pieces to keep, and which to trade off.

If you have a couple of extra pawns, the easiest win usually comes by trading off all of the pieces except pawns. The kings must remain, of course. On the other hand, if the game is fairly close, you have to decide how to make the most of your position.

All pieces can be good defenders. Suppose you have one pawn and a bishop left. Your opponent has only a bishop. If your opponent can sacrifice that bishop for your pawn, you are left with an unwinnable endgame of just bishop vs. king, where there are no possible checkmates. This is a great defensive technique.

In the endgame, you should ask yourself how useful your pieces can be, given the location of enemy pawns. A bishop in a strong position can be worth a rook. When one of Black's hanging pawns advances, White's bishop turns into a monster. Bishops in particular are sensitive to pawn structures. Observe how they interact in this game.

**1.c4.** Fischer was a devotee of 1.e4 and rarely strayed. For his World Championship challenge he decided to use the English Opening. **1...e6.** This defense, sometimes known as the Agincourt Defense, is used by Black to more or less force the game into a standard Queen's Gambit Declined. Black will next advance the pawn to d5. White usually puts a pawn at d4 to prevent the Black pawn from advancing further.

**2.Nf3.** After 2.d4, Fischer would have many choices. He could have switched back to a Nimzo-Indian approach with 2...Nf6, perhaps later switching to a Benoni (...c5) or Queen's Gambit (...d5). It is unlikely that the Kangaroo (2...Bb4+) would have hopped on the World Championship board, but we'll never know. **2...d5; 3.d4.** So, the Queen's Gambit it is. 3...Nf6. Fischer was not a fan of Tarrasch's 3...c5. **4.Nc3 Be7; 5.Bg5 O-O; 6.e3.**

The game follows the traditional pattern. Both sides develop their forces quickly, not aiming for early attacks against the enemy king.

**6...h6.** A useful move, because it not only kicks out an enemy invader, but also makes a little escape square for the king. **7.Bh4.** Fischer liked bishops and was not inclined to exchange his for the knight at f6. **7...b6.** Savielly Tartakower's plan, which has been a major defensive plan for a long time. Black will fianchetto the bishop at b7, and then can open a line for the bishop by exchanging his pawn at d5 for the White pawn at c4. **8.cxd5.**

**8...Nxd5.** Black captures with the knight, because it will be able to get out of the way, once the bishop lands at b7. **9.Bxe7.** This trade foils Black's strategy, to some extent. **9...Qxe7.** Capturing with the knight is considered inferior. 9...Nxe7; 10.Bd3 Bb7; 11.Rc1! leaves Black with some problems on the c-file.

**10.Nxd5 exd5.** It seems that the bishop won't have much of a future at b7, but now it can easily move out along the c8-h3 diagonal. **11.Rc1.** It still makes sense for White to work along the c-file. However, Black will be able to advance the pawn from c7 to c5, where it can be well supported. **11...Be6.**

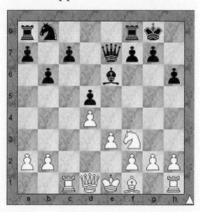

This looks like a passive position for the bishop, but for the moment it defends the pawn and allows Black to get a rook to c8. Black could have gotten queens off the board with 11...Qb4+; 12.Qd2

Qxd2+; 13.Kxd2 but that endgame is miserable for Black due to pressure on the c-file, a more central king, and much more useful bishop.

**12.Qa4 c5; 13.Qa3.** White pins the pawn at c5, adding to the pressure. Black is prepared, however. **13...Rc8; 14.Bb5.** Fischer uses the plan designed by the Soviet star Semyon Furman. It is not really superior to simply placing the bishop at e2. At b5, it can be chased away by ...a6. Black should be careful about the timing of the move, however.

**14...a6.** A bit too automatic. Spassky needed to be a bit bolder. 14...Qb7! is the correct move. It is a pawn sacrifice, introduced the following year in a game between Jan Timman and Yefim Geller. 15.dxc5 bxc5; 16.Rxc5 Rxc5; 17.Qxc5 Na6. Black has a strong initiative, and White's game quickly fell apart. **15.dxc5 bxc5; 16.O-O.**

White finally castles, but late castling is typical in the old Queen's Gambit because Black has no way of getting at White's king early in the game. We now have the famous "hanging pawn" position. Black's pawns are not easy to defend, because there are no neighboring pawns to help out. At the same time, however, they control four very important squares and limit White's scope of operations in the center of the board. Such unbalanced pawn structures have both strengths and weaknesses. It is important to know how to handle these positions, but it is a rather advanced topic. You'll see a few of the main ideas illustrated in this game.

**16...Ra7?!** In some ways, this is a very natural move, unpinning the a-pawn and allowing the rook to get to the center. This plan turns out to be insufficient to obtain equality for Black. 16...Qa7!?; 17.Ba4 a5!; 18.Qb3 Nd7; 19.Bxd7 Qxd7 is correct, as was later demonstrated in a game between Makarychev vs. Sturua, played in 1979. **17.Be2 Nd7.** This is actually the first new move of the game! 17...a5; 18.Rc3 Nd7; 19.Rfc1 Re8; 20.Bb5 Bg4; 21.Nd2 d4; 22.exd4 cxd4; 23.Qxe7 Rxe7; 24.Rc8+ gave White a great position in the game Furman vs. Geller, 1970. So Bobby was putting the "enemy" Russian ideas to good use! **18.Nd4!**

Fischer exploits the pin on the c-pawn to bring the knight to a powerful position. It can later go to b3, adding yet another attacker to the battle at c5.

**18...Qf8.** The queen retreats so that she is defended. Both of White's pins are broken, now that the rook at c8 is defended, too. 18...Nf6 was the consensus choice of the analysts after the game. Former World Champion Mikhail Tal contributed to the discussion. 19.Nb3 Nd7; 20.Rc3 was evaluated by Tal as better for White. **19.Nxe6 fxe6; 20.e4!**

The moment of truth has arrived. The pressure on the pawns has built to the point where one of them simply must move forward. This is what the holder of hanging pawns hates most. The pawns should only be advanced when the advance has a great effect. Once one pawn advances, it's companion is left as a backward pawn, which is usually very weak. So by forcing one of the pawns to move forward, Fischer gains a position and a psychological victory.

**20...d4?** The wrong choice. True, leaving the pawns in place would lead to trouble, but it was the c-pawn that should have stepped forward.

20...dxe4 leaves both e-pawns very weak. White's bishop can use the extra space. 21.Qe3! Qf5; 22.Rc4 Nf6; 23.Rfc1 Rac7; 24.R1c2 followed by ...Qc1, and soon both the c-pawn and a-pawn will fall.

20...c4 was best, though White would still have a lot of pressure after 21.Qh3 Qf7; 22.Bg4 Re8; 23.exd5 exd5; 24.Rfe1 Rxe1+; 25.Rxe1 Nf8 as analyzed by Tal.

**21.f4.** White has a substantial advantage. The White pawns, which are easily supported, are strong. Black now suffers from a backward pawn at c5. **21...Qe7; 22.e5! Rb8.** The best chance. White is prevented from playing Qb3, pinning the pawn at e6 and creating the threat of advancing the f-pawn to f5. **23.Bc4!**

One backward pawn is blockaded and another is pinned. In addition, a third week pawn is attacked! Quite an achievement for a single move! **23...Kh8.** On 23...Nb6, White would have been able to obtain a great game with 24.Qb3. Tal pointed out that this is much stronger than grabbing the weakling at c5, though that would also be in White's favor.

**24.Qh3 Nf8.** If Black captures at b2, he finds himself in a lost endgame. 24...Rxb2; 25.Qxe6! Qxe6; 26.Bxe6 and Black's connected passed pawns are easy to stop. For example, 26...d3; 27.Rfd1 d2; 28.Ra1. **25.b3 a5; 26.f5**.

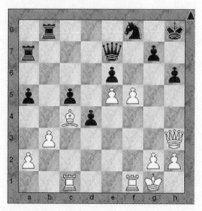

The opening of the f-file spells doom for Black. **26...exf5; 27.Rxf5 Nh7.** Spassky sets a little trap. If Bobby infiltrates with the rook, then 28...Ng5 will be an embarrassing fork. In addition, if the pawn advances to e6, Spassky can plant the knight at f6 and set up a solid defense.

**28.Rcf1!** Bobby doesn't fall for such tricks. He knows that Black's position is so passive, and the pawns are so weak, that he can patiently build up the position. **28...Qd8; 29.Qg3 Re7; 30.h4!**

This takes away the only square available to the knight, which is now in complete exile on the rim. **30...Rbb7; 31.e6 Rbc7; 32.Qe5 Qe8.** 32...d3; 33.R5f3 d2; 34.Rd3 would also have put an end to Spassky's hopes.

**33.a4!** Black is running out of moves. **33...Qd8; 34.R1f2 Qe8; 35.R2f3 Qd8; 36.Bd3 Qe8; 37.Qe4!** This sets up a nasty checkmating trick at h7. The game is effectively over. **37...Nf6.**

Time for a little sacrifice to destroy the barrier. **38.Rxf6! gxf6; 39.Rxf6.** It is fitting that the point of this exchange sacrifice is to further weaken Black's pawns! Since these pawns guard the king, it is easy for Fischer to finish him off. **39...Kg8; 40.Bc4 Kh8; 41.Qf4.**

Black **resigned**. Checkmate can't be postponed for more than eight moves. White doesn't even have to go after the h-pawn, but can just set up unstoppable threats by playing Qe5.

**Game notes:** After losing the first game of the match, and forfeiting the second in a dispute, Fischer managed to pull even after five games. In this dramatic sixth game, Fischer took the lead, and never looked back. Winning with the Black pieces added psychological value to his victory.

# DEATH ON THE DIAGONALS

**THE PLAYERS**
Bobby Fischer (White)
vs.
Boris Spassky (U.S.S.R.)

**THE LOCATION**
The World Championship Match,
in Reykjavik, Iceland,
on 7/27/1972

## LESSON: ENEMY PIECES CAN BE TRAPPED BY DISTANT WARRIORS

When you are concerned with the safety of your pieces, you always want to make sure they are not under attack by pieces of lesser value. It doesn't take long to learn that pieces can be attacked at great distance by bishops, rooks and queens.

It is harder to notice that far off opposition can conspire to trap your pieces even on their home squares. As pawns advance, lines are opened. Not necessarily for rooks on the ranks, but often for bishops that can suddenly get to previously inaccessible squares. Every time you advance a pawn, it creates a small weakness. The further the pawn advances, the more weak squares are left in its wake. A pawn defended by another pawn is usually a very strong barrier, but only as long as the pawns remain in place.

Before advancing pawns, especially two squares, take a look at your opponent's bishops and see if they can do any additional damage if the pawns are moved.

**1.c4 c5; 2.Nc3 Nc6; 3.Nf3 Nf6; 4.g3 g6; 5.Bg2 Bg7; 6.O-O O-O.**

The symmetrical variation of the English Opening is a flexible formation. Both sides have the option to place a pawn in the center at almost any time, though they can also develop more modestly. In this game, White decides to grab a piece of the center.

**7.d4.** Naturally Bobby chooses the most aggressive continuation. **7...cxd4; 8.Nxd4 Nxd4; 9.Qxd4 d6; 10.Bg5.** Fischer explores less familiar territory than the then-common 10.Qd3.

**10...Be6.** It is more common for Black to kick the bishop with ... h6. Fischer doesn't give Spassky a second chance. **11.Qf4.** Black was threatening to move the knight to d5, exposing the queen to attack. So Bobby shifts it, also stopping Black from kicking the bishop. He also prepares to infiltrate at h6 when convenient. **11... Qa5.** Black should probably have chosen ...Rab8 immediately.

**12.Rac1**. Both sides have almost completed development. The rooks can see each other, and all that remains is to centralize one of them and then attacks can be launched. The rook moves to protect the knight, so that White can later play b3, supporting the pawn at c4. **12...Rab8; 13.b3 Rfc8; 14.Qd2 a6; 15.Be3**.

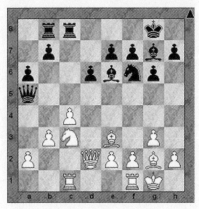

Both sides have completed development, so maneuvering and repositioning pieces is not a waste of time. It isn't clear how Black should proceed, but there is general agreement that Spassky over-reached a bit with his next move.

**15...b5?** It is clear that Black must play on the queenside, but commentators were quick to offer a whole slew of alternatives. The problem with the move is that it opens up the long diagonal, so that the White bishop at g2 becomes even more powerful. 15...Rc7;

16.Rfd1 Rbc8 would bring equality, according to Svetozar Gligoric, a strong Grandmaster. 15...Bd7; 16.Ba7 Ra8; 17.Bd4 Bc6; 18.e4 b5 was a different path to a level game, proposed by Smyslov. 15...Qh5 was proposed by Salo Flohr, one of the top players in his time.

**16.Ba7! bxc4**. Spassky of course did not overlook the loss of his rook for the enemy bishop. He felt that his pressure on the queenside would be sufficient compensation. However, it turns out that the exchange sacrifice is a bad strategy in this position, as White has more resources than might appear at first glance. 16...Ra8 would yield the rook to White's other bishop. It might seem logical to want to get rid of the light square bishop, but in fact White's dark square bishop could then retreat to take up a powerful post at d4.

**17.Bxb8 Rxb8; 18.bxc4 Bxc4; 19.Rfd1**. Surely both sides were able to calculate this position back when Spassky played 15...b5.

I suspect that Spassky, when he actually reached this position, knew that his strategy had failed, and perhaps that explains his blunder on the next move.

**19...Nd7??** Black's position is in bad shape, but Spassky's choice is suicidal. The queen should have moved, perhaps to e5 or h5. **20.Nd5!** Because Black's bishop at c4 is still under attack, this move is simply devastating. All Spassky can do now is try to find the path of greatest resistance. Perhaps his morale was broken, but he rolled over like a circus animal.

**20...Qxd2?** This leads by force to an endgame so bad that no player in their right mind should even consider it. But what else was there? **21.Nxe7+ Kf8; 22.Rxd2 Kxe7; 23.Rxc4 Rb1+; 24.Bf1.**

White is up the exchange (rook for knight) and has a better pawn structure. As this was a World Championship match, Spassky bravely fought on, but the situation is already hopeless.

**24...Nc5; 25.Kg2 a5!** If there is any hope, it lies on the a-file. **26.e4 Ba1.** This is played to keep the bishop alive after Black plays ...f6, which will be necessary in the battle over e5. **27.f4 f6; 28.Re2 Ke6; 29.Rec2 Bb2; 30.Be2 h5?!** The weakening of the kingside was not needed, though Black is unlikely to survive in any case. **31.Rd2 Ba3.**

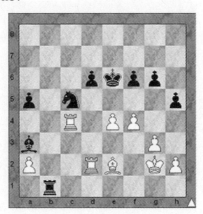

The only question here is whether Spassky can survive to reach time control at move 40, adjourn the game and resign out of public sight. Fischer shows no compassion and finishes off the game efficiently.

**32.f5+! gxf5; 33.exf5+ Ke5**. 33...Kxf5; 34.Rxc5+! dxc5; 35.Bd3+ Ke5; 36.Bxb1 with an extra rook for White. **34.Rcd4 Kxf5; 35.Rd5+ Ke6; 36.Rxd6+ Ke7; 37.Rc6**. Black **resigned**.

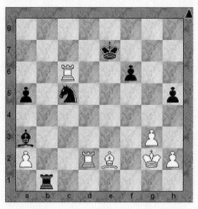

Although down only an exchange, Black will now lose the h-pawn, and White's h-pawn will become a queen before too long.

**Game notes:** This game shows Fischer using a standard fork trick to trip up a World Champion and consolidate his lead in the match! This time he has White, but the game starts out quietly. Fischer knew that a win would bring his lead to two points, but a loss would return to a level match. The pressure was on!

# GAME
# #24

# CAUGHT UNAWARE

## THE PLAYERS

Bobby Fischer (White)
vs.
Boris Spassky (France)

## THE LOCATION

The "World Champion Rematch,"
in Sveti-Stefan, Yugoslavia,
on 9/2/1992

## LESSON: ATTACKING DOESN'T NEED QUEENS!

Although queens are the Amazon warriors of the chessboard, it is quite possible to attack without them. When there is a vulnerable enemy king, especially when there is castling on opposite flanks, the rooks, bishops and knights, aided by a few pawns, can get the job done just as well.

A successful attack is more likely when the opponent has forces that can't get into defensive positions. When all the pieces are properly developed, it is difficult to attack without queens. Getting past the king's natural pawn barrier will often require a little sacrifice. Sacrificing is easier when the opponent has offside pieces because it is almost as if they don't count.

A battle against the king is like its own little war. For a brief time, the rest of the world doesn't matter. If you have enough attacking force to smash through defensive barriers before reinforcements can arise then it makes no difference how many pieces have to be sacrificed. As long as there is enough left to finish off the enemy king!

**1.e4 e5; 2.Nf3 Nc6; 3.Bb5 a6; 4.Bxc6.**

The Exchange Variation is considered a major part of Fischer's opening repertoire, and his advocacy of the line has been used to promote the Exchange Variation in various publications. In reality, he just used it from time to time, and was generally more comfortable imposing the usual Spanish Torture in the Closed Variation. In this particular game he was very well prepared, and unleashed a new move that simply demolished Spassky's position.

**4...dxc6; 5.O-O f6.** This move would be odd in most circumstances, but in the Exchange Spanish it is almost inevitable.

Black has to support the e5-square, whether or not the pawn at e5 is exchanged for a White one at d4. There is therefore no reason not

to play it right away. Notice that the usual trick at e5 does not work here. **6.Nxe5? fxe5; 7.Qh5+ Kd7** and despite the exposed position of the Black king, White cannot successfully conclude the attack.

**6.d4 exd4; 7.Nxd4 c5.** This lets Black swap queens. Then in the endgame the bishops can be effective. A good plan, but the attack does not end when the queens leave the playing field! **8.Nb3 Qxd1; 9.Rxd1.** White has a pawn majority on the kingside, and this can be decisive in some endgames. Black has the bishop pair, which can wreak havoc in the middlegame if enough lines are opened. **9...Bg4; 10.f3 Be6.** Black provoked the weakness of the a7-g1 diagonal with this maneuver. **11.Nc3 Bd6; 12.Be3 b6.**

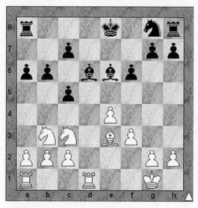

Black's clerics are remarkably silent. Yet at the time this game was played, the position was considered quite reasonable.

**13.a4.** Now, according to Kasparov, Spassky should have played 13...Kf7 with equal chances. The brilliant tactician and theoretician Leonid Shamkovich points out that 13...a5 might also be playable. Shamkovich is probably right, since Spassky digs his own grave by allowing the White pawn to reach a5 at the next move. **13...O-O-O.** The books had said this was a fine move, but Fischer proves otherwise. **14.a5 Kb7.**

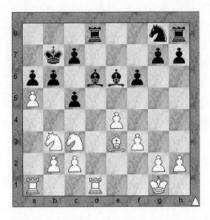

The whole point of the formation with pawn at f6 and bishop at d6 is to prevent the White pawn from reaching e5. Bobby Fischer is not so easily denied! **15.e5!!** The first sign of serious trouble for Black. The pawn cannot be taken. Curiously, this is not the first time this position has been reached. We are still in known territory. **15...Be7.** 15...fxe5; 16.axb6 cxb6; 17.Ne4 Bc7 and White can win material with a small sacrifice. 18.Nbxc5+ bxc5; 19.Nxc5+ Kc8; 20.Rxd8+ Bxd8; 21.Nxe6 is gruesome.

**16.Rxd8 Bxd8.**

**17.Ne4.** An improvement on 17.axb6 cxb6, which had been seen back in 1976. Now Spassky blunders away the game, yet we are still following a game that was over a decade old at the time. Spassky is a creative genius, but has never been known as a particularly hard worker, especially in the opening.

**17...Kc6??** Spassky later said "I was thinking about 17...Bd5 and could find no advantage for White, when I suddenly got the idea to play 17...Kc6. Of course I could immediately see that in two moves, I was lost."

17...Bxb3; 18.cxb3 f5; 19.Rd1 Ne7; 20.Ng5 Nc6; 21.axb6 Bxg5; 22.Bxg5 Kxb6; 23.Rd7 Re8; 24.Rxg7 Rxe5 ;25.Rxh7 Re1+; 26.Kf2 Rb1; 27.h4 gave White a substantial advantage in a 1980 game played by Fischer's friend Peter Biyiasas as White. Fischer may have known the game from Biyiasas, or may have read about it in a 1992 book on the opening by Grandmaster Andrew Soltis, in which considerable analysis of the position was published.

**18.axb6 cxb6.** Now the heavily defended pawn at c5 is blown away. **19.Nbxc5! Bc8.** Capturing the knight leads to the loss of a piece. 19...bxc5; 20.Rxa6+ Kd7; 21.Nxc5+ Ke7; 22.Nxe6 g6; 23.Bc5+ Ke8; 24.Ra8 and White wins the bishop. **20.Nxa6 fxe5; 21.Nb4+.** Black **resigned.**

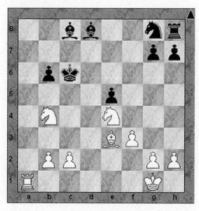

White has an extra pawn, and Black's pieces are useless. The main threat is Ra8 with devastation on the home ranks. So the king has to retreat. The knights will continue the attack, and the position is not worth defending. Notice that Black's kingside pieces never moved!

**Game notes:** The whole world watched Fischer's 1992 rematch with Spassky, even though it didn't have any official status. His convincing victory over Spassky, who never fully recovered from the 1972 defeat, is the last we've heard of Bobby at the board. Ever since his retirement, rumors have circulated about his return. It seems unlikely he will ever play competitive chess again, but you never know.

ENDGAME
WISDOM

## ENDGAME #1

# USING A DISTANT PAWN AS A DECOY

**THE PLAYERS**
Bobby Fischer (White)
vs.
Bent Larsen (Denmark)

**THE LOCATION**
World Championship Candidates
Match, at Denver (USA),
in 1971

## LESSON: USING PASSED PAWNS AS WEAPONS

When you have a passed pawn on the edge of the board you will usually want to concentrate on moving it forward so that it can be promoted. However, there is another good use for such pawns. You can use them to lure enemy defenders of the other flank to the opposite side so that they can deal with the pawn.

This is illustrated most clearly in king and pawn endgames. It is equally useful in knight endgames and can also be very helpful in the bishop endgames, as Bobby Fischer shows here in his ascent to the World Championship.

Fischer demonstrates simple winning technique for such positions. Get rid of the bishops and use the a-pawn to keep the Black king busy while going after the kingside pawns.

**38.a4! Kf8; 39.Bc3!** The correct decision to exchange bishops leads to a winning king and pawn endgame for White. 39.Bb6?! Ke7; 40.a5 Kd7; 41.a6 Kc6; 42.a7 Kb7. Black will be able to draw if he can get rid of the kingside pawns, even if he has to sacrifice his bishop. Black's king can never be evicted from the corner.

**39...Bxc3.** Black has no choice. 39...Ba3; 40.a5 Bc5; 41.a6. and White will win after Bd4. **40.Kxc3 Ke7; 41.Kd4**. Fischer brings his king to the kingside to gobble Black's pawns. Larsen cannot defend them because he has to deal with the passed pawn on the opposite flank. This is a standard winning method in king and pawn endgames.

**41...Kd6; 42.a5 f6.** Now White must use the queenside pawn as a decoy so that his king can gain access to Black's pawns. **43.a6! Kc6; 44.a7 Kb7; 45.Kd5 h4; 46.Ke6.** Black resigned. All the kingside pawns will be lost except for one pawn, which is sufficient to win. The Black king is simply too far away.

# FACEOFF IN HAVANA

**THE PLAYERS**
Bobby Fischer (White)
vs.
Istvan Bilek (Hungary)

**THE LOCATION**
Capablanca Memorial,
Havana (Cuba),
in 1965

## LESSON: QUEEN OR TWO ROOKS?

In the endgame, two rooks can often outplay a queen because they can join together and cover a great deal of territory. The more pawns on the board, the better the chances for the queen because she can move to attacking positions easily. The queen should be kept mobile and pawns should be used to make progress.

This game presents an excellent example of how to do that.

Queen against two rooks is never easy, but White's extra pawns are powerful and provide the path to victory. Fischer uses the h-pawn to tie down the rooks, then the pawns go to work.

**29.Qh8 Re7.** Black has no useful moves. **30.h6 Kf7.** Black hopes to use the king to confront the racing pawn.

**31.Qh7+ Kf8; 32.Qd3!** Getting out of the way of the pawn. **32... Kf7; 33.h7!** Passed pawns must be pushed! **33...Rh5.** This rook becomes overworked, having to cover the h-file and f5. **33... Kg7??** loses to **34.h8=Q+! Kxh8; 35.Qd8+. 34.Qd5+ Re6.** Walking into a pin, but there was nothing better.

**35.f4!** Fischer threatens the deadly f5! **35...f5; 36.fxe5!** The advanced pawn is sacrificed to deflect the rook. **36...Rxh7.**

**37.Qd7+ Re7.** Forced. **38.Qxf5+.** White now has connected passed pawns and the win is easy. **38...Ke8; 39.f4 Kd8; 40.e6.** Black resigned. There is no stopping the pawns.

# ENDGAME #3

# BISHOP POWER

**THE PLAYERS**

Bobby Fischer (White)
vs.
Pal Benko (Hungary)

**THE LOCATION**

Candidates Tournament,
Curacao (Netherlands Antilles),
1962

## LESSON: BISHOPS OF OPPOSITE COLORS WITH ROOKS

Bishops of opposite colors provide a lot of drawing chances when they are accompanied by mere pawns, but the addition of other pieces allows them to become attacking weapons. If you have the advantage, it is wise to try to eliminate the bishops and reduce the drawing chances for your opponent. If you're on the weaker side, then you should try to maintain the bishops of opposite color and get rid of the other pieces.

Fischer has an extra pawn, but there are bishops of opposite color, so Fischer can't operate on the queenside alone. He needs to get bishops off the board while making the a-pawn a passed pawn. Black should be trying to exchange rooks and must play actively.

**23...g6?** A very bad move, since White exploits the g6-square. 23... Rad8 was better. Fischer still might have won eventually. **24.Bd3 Rad8.** 24...b4!?; 25.h5 Kg7; 26.Rh3 prepares to double rooks on the h-file. 26...gxh5; 27.Rxh5 h6. It is not easy to find a winning plan for White, who needs to get both rooks involved.

**25.h5!** Pouring on the pressure at g6. 25.Bxb5 Rb8; 26.Rd5 a6!; 27.Bc4 Rxb2+; 28.Kc1 Rb4; 29.Bxa6 Ra8; 30.Rb5! Rd4; 31.Rb6 Bxh4 should lead to a draw. **25...Kg7; 26.hxg6 hxg6; 27.Bxb5.** Fischer grabs an additional pawn, but a pair of rooks come off.

**27...Rxd1+; 28.Rxd1 Rb8.** Looks like Black is going to get the pawn back at b2. **29.a4 a6!** This demands that Fischer plays accurately. White wants bishops off the board, then the queenside pawns will win in the rook ending. **30.Rd7+!** Masterful precision nudges the king away from the bishop. **30...Kh6; 31.Rd6!** Black has to give up the a-pawn or adopt desperate measures.

**31...Bxb2!?** 31...axb5; 32.Rxf6 bxa4; 33.Rf4 a3; 34.b4 is an easy win after the king picks off the a-pawn. **32.Kxb2 axb5.** Black is just one pawn down in the rook ending, but his king is way offside. **33.a5!** 33.axb5 Rxb5+ will likely be drawn as Black's rook goes after the g-pawn and, if necessary, can be sacrificed for White's remaining pawn.

**33...Ra8; 34.a6 Kh5.**

**35.Kb3.** Now the White king takes over as escort for the pawn. **35...g5; 36.Kb4 Kg4; 37.Kxb5 Kg3; 38.Rd7 g4; 39.a7.** Black resigned because the king will walk to b7.

# KNIGHT POWER

**THE PLAYERS**
Bobby Fischer (White)
vs.
Wolfgang Unzicker (Germany)

**THE LOCATION**
The Olympiad
at Siegen (Germany),
1970

## LESSON: USE KNIGHT FORKS IN ENDGAMES

Knights are excellent infiltrators and they can use forks and threats of forks to force the opponent to advance pawns. As pawns advance, they become weaker and create holes in the position, which can be used for further infiltrations. Because knights can use all 64 squares, unlike bishops, they are especially useful in the endgames with weak pawns.

When you have a night against the bishop in the endgame, you should try to infiltrate with the knight and provoke weaknesses that can be exploited later.

Fischer displays the power of the knight fork in the endgame, causing all sorts of problems for his opponent. Fischer wins a pawn tactically, but exploiting the advantage is not so simple. **36.Nd5.**

**36...Bc6**. 36...Kg7 makes more sense. Bringing the knight to e5 would be helpful. Still, White should win. **37.Nxc7 Bf3**. Black's plan is to win the g-pawn, but that is not going to happen. **38.Ne8!** Setting up a fork at f6 if Black captures at g4.

**38...Kh6; 39.Nf6!** Heading to d7 to go after queenside pawns. **39...Kg7.** 39...Bc6 dominates the knight, but it can escape via h5 and g3. 40.Kf2 Kg7; 41.Nh5+ Kf7; 42.Ke3 followed by Ng3 and Ne4, forcing trade of minor pieces, after which the king and pawn endgame is simple. **40.Kf2 Bd1; 41.Nd7! c4.** 41...Bxg4; 42.f6+ Kg8; 43.f7+ Kxf7 allows the fork 44.Ne5+. **42.Kg3!** Black resigned. The pawn at g4 is defended and the queenside pawns will start to fall to the knight.

# ENDGAME #5 ZUGZWANG

**THE PLAYERS**
Bobby Fischer (White)
vs.
Taimanov M.

**THE LOCATION**
Quarterfinal Candidates Match
in Vancouver (Canada),
1971

## LESSON: ZUGZWANG PRESSURE

An important truth in the endgame is the concept of zugzwang. That is the situation when a player is forced to move and suffers as a result, but where no harm would come if the player could just pass. This is especially important in king and pawn endgames, but can also be applied in a variety of situations. A key element in bringing about zugzwang situations is pressure.

Putting pressure on the enemy position is useful in all aspects of the game but is especially useful in endgames. If a piece is under pressure, it cannot be captured safely right away. In the endgame, where there are a few pieces on the board, having a piece tied down to defense is unpleasant. Bishops and rooks are especially useful because they can apply pressure from a great distance. Most players do not appreciate the usefulness of pressure and don't look for opportunities to establish it. You should try to think about pressure points throughout the game, but especially in the endgame where a little bit of pressure can lead to victory.

**54.Bb3!** Fischer had to find a way to get his bishop to a long diagonal. **54...Ka7.** There is nothing better. 54...Nc8; 55.Bd5+ Kc7; 56.Ka6. White wins. **55.Bd1!** Headed for f3. **55...Kb7; 56.Bf3+ Kc7.** 56...Ka7; 57.Bg2 and White wins. **57.Ka6 Ng8; 58.Bd5.** The bishop dominates the board and must be chased from this fantastic post.

**58...Ne7.** 58...Nf6; 59.Bf7 Ne4; 60.Bxg6 Nxg3; 61.c4! Kc6; 62.Ka7 Kc7; 63.Bf7 was demonstrated by Taimanov. More pawns must fall. **59.Bc4! Nc6.** 59...Kc6; 60.Bb5+ Kc7; 61.Be8 Kd8. White wins with the same tactic we'll see in the game. The bishop will be sacrificed at g6. **60.Bf7.** The invasion of the ever vulnerable square puts enormous pressure on the kingside, tying down the knight. **60...Ne7; 61.Be8!** Zugzwang. **61...Kd8.** Now comes a winning shot! **62.Bxg6!! Nxg6; 63.Kxb6.** Fischer plans to win on the queenside.

**63...Kd7.** 63...Ne7; 64.Kxa5 and White wins. 63...Nf8; 64.Kxa5 Kc7; 65.Kb5 Ne6; 66.a5 Kb7; 67.a6+ Ka7; 68.Kc4! Kxa6; 69.Kd5 Nd8; 70.Kxc5. This is a win for White because the king can run over to the kingside and grab the pawns. The only way for Black to defend would be to get the knight to g3, but that's not possible in time. 70...Nf7; 71.Kd5 Nh6; 72.Ke5 Kb5; 73.Kf6 Kc4; 74.Kg6 Ng4; 75.Kxh5 Kb3; 76.Kg5 Ne3; 77.h5 etc. **64.Kxc5 Ne7; 65.b4!** Creating connected passed pawns.

**65...axb4; 66.cxb4 Nc8; 67.a5.**

**67...Nd6.** 67...Kc7; 68.b5 Ne7; 69.b6+ and White wins. **68.b5 Ne4+; 69.Kb6!** The king escorts the a-pawn. **69...Kc8; 70.Kc6 Kb8.** 70...Nxg3; 71.a6 Kb8; 72.b6 Ne4; 73.a7+ Ka8; 74.b7+ Kxa7; 75.Kc7 and White wins. **71.b6.** Black resigned. White will get a new queen. The knight can't help because the White king covers c5 and d6.

# ENDGAME #6

## PATHWAYS AND OPPORTUNITIES

**THE PLAYERS**
Arpad Elo (USA)
vs.
Bobby Fischer (Black)

**THE LOCATION**
Milwaukee (USA),
1957

## LESSON: ROADBLOCKS

The endgame is all about pathways. Usually, you are trying to build roads from your pawn positions to their promotions squares. At other times you seek opportunities for your king or pieces to infiltrate the enemy positions. The flip side of this is that you must keep your opponent from accomplishing these goals. To do this it is important to control key squares that can be used as a pathway.

If the road is going to be a straight one, then rooks are best equipped to seal them off. If it is a diagonal line, then you want to use your bishops to prevent infiltration, or sometimes knights. If you can succeed in building your roadway while the opponent's path is blocked you will likely win the game. So in the endgame, ask yourself this: Is there any way my opponent can infiltrate my position? If so, try to find a way to stop that from happening.

**42.c4? Kd4! 43.Kg4.** White hopes to go after the kingside pawns. It is not going to happen. **43...Bg6!** Black eliminates all entrance squares.

**44.Kf3.** White needs to guard e4 with the king or the pawn will be captured, **44...Bh5+; 45.Kf2 Bd1!** Now the bishop will go after the queenside pawn. **46.Kg3 Be2.** To prevent the White king from getting to f3 to defend the pawn.

**47.c5??** White panics. 47.Kf2 Bxc4; 48.Bb7 Bd3; 49.Kf3 would have kept alive hopes for a draw. **47...Kxc5; 48.Be6 Kd4.** Fittingly, the Black king returns to the central square made available by White's initial blunder. **49.Bf5 Ke3.** White resigned because the remaining pawn will fall.

# ENDGAME #7

# ROOK ENDGAME

**THE PLAYERS**
Bobby Fischer (White)
vs.
James Sherwin (USA)

**THE LOCATION**
Interzonal Tournament,
Portoroz (Slovenia),
1958

## LESSON: BUILDING A BRIDGE

In endgames, there are certain techniques that you absolutely must know because they are difficult to discover for yourself at the chessboard. An important trick in rook endgames is called building a bridge. This technique is used in endgames that feature a rook and pawn against a rook. It is often necessary to shelter your king behind a rook to protect it from checks, and to allow the pawn to promote.

In our example, Fischer's opponent resigned before the bridge building took place, but we can examine the final position and see how it works.

**76.Rf5 Ra4; 77.Rf8 Ke7; 78.Rf3 Ke6?** The king is a fool! He needs to be on defense against the g-pawn, not an aggressor. 78...Ra8; 79.g5 Rf8; 80.Ra3 Kf7 is the correct strategy. 81.Rf3+ Kg7 is headed for a draw. **79.Kh4! Ra8; 80.g5! Rh8+; 81.Kg4 Ke7; 82.g6 Rf8; 83.Rf5 Rh8.** 83...Rxf5; 84.Kxf5 Ke8; 85.Ke6! Opposition! 85...Kf8; 86.Kf6 Kg8; 87.g7 Kh7; 88.Kf7 wins. **84.Kg5 Rh1; 85.Rf2 Rh3; 86.g7 Rg3+; 87.Kh6 Rh3+ 88.Kg6 Rg3+; 89.Kh7 Rh3+; 90.Kg8.** Black resigned.

The winning technique for White is part of any experienced player's arsenal. 90...Rh1; 91.Rf4. Fischer now would have used the technique called "building a bridge." He maneuvers the rook into a position where it will eventually be able to block the last enemy check and secure the promotion of the pawn. At the right time, White will check on the e-file to force the enemy king further away. 91...Rh2; 92.Re4+ Kd6; 93.Kf7 Rf2+; 94.Kg6 Rg2+; 95.Kf6 Rf2+; 96.Kg5 Rg2+; 97.Rg4. The pawn promotes.